My Music is done, What's next?

The Promoter's Almanac

By
Barron Smith

S.O.S
FILMS
PUBLISHING
MUSIC
ENT.

S.O.S Entertainment ™
10346 Ittner Dr.
St. Louis, MO 63136
www.smit-t.com
314-517-5739

First published by S.O.S Entertainment 12/28/2010

ISBN – 13: 978-1-4538907-1-4
ISBN – 10: 1-4538907-1-8

Printed in the United States of America

Visit our website at: www.smit-t.com

Table of Contents

JHowes Management – A Premier Management/ Promotion Company in St. Louis

Promoting

People promote themselves as well as other things on a daily basis whether they realize it or not. These things can include but are not limited to the clothes you wear to the car you drive. Have you ever gone into a restaurant and the food was so great that you couldn't wait to tell someone else?

Well guess what, you just helped promote that establishment. In most cases, you endorsed it better than the owner because you have a personal experience. Even if you didn't like your visit your promotion would be drastically different.

Promoting is an easy thing to do especially when it's in your favor. We just need to learn how to advertise ourselves. Think about the fashion world, they have promoting down to an art. They take your favorite artists and provide them with free clothing, so when you see them in concert or videos they're wearing the designers' garments.

They may even say the designers name in their song. So even if you don't see them when you buy their music you'll hear about their clothing line. Having a clothing line is so major that even artists have their own brand of clothes.

Hip-hop has a multitude of companies endorsing certain artists such as Queen Latifah with Maybelline to 50 Cent with Vitamin Water. These companies are opting for a vast array of artists to help sponsor their products. In doing so, they are able to reach a wider audience.

To be a hip-hop artist in today's world entails more than just selling records; the doors are open to many business opportunities. Remember when making music was the easy part because no one could tell you how to craft your style? But where most people made their mistake was in promoting. I've always wondered why a lot of underground artists never had a successful career.

The talent is there, but getting their product out is where they lacked. Promotion is a strategic game. You have to make people want your product. We had an artist that would always be out giving his cd to people.

He would give his cd to anyone, he didn't care if they were old, blind, or a different nationality. One of his friends told him that he was wasting his time giving his cd to that old man. This particular artist would always counter with: "You don't know if he has children or grandchildren that he can give the cd to."

NOW THAT'S A GREAT PROMOTION TECHNIQUE! If you make excuses for promoting, than people will make excuses for not purchasing your product. You can't limit yourself or your product when it comes to promoting. Let people decide if they don't want to buy or support your product. Don't discredit them because you feel they're not going to buy it.

Remember, there's no one that will promote your material better than you. You can be the best at what you do, but it doesn't matter if no one knows about your product. Promoting should be your second language especially if you're selling something.

Even if you have people helping you to show support, don't slack up, the more people that contribute, the better the outcome.

As I mentioned before about our artist, every time I mentioned his name people would say, "I know him, he gave me a cd."

It works; you just have to apply yourself. We're in a competitive society where everyone rap, sing and produce. You have to figure out a way to stand in front and to be marketable to people. Come up with a good sales pitch without being annoying.

A person will buy your product if they have the money and if they feel that you are confident about your product. Also, make sure your product is presentable.

If it's a cd, make sure it has an insert and is packaged correctly. One of my biggest pet peeves is getting a cd from an artist with no info on the cd.

That's very unprofessional and it shows that you don't care enough about your product. SO WHY SHOULD I CARE?

Many times, people judge you off of your material. You must invest in yourself if you want people to take you serious.

If you need something to make your product better, THAN GET IT! Don't settle for less. If you're able to make money off of your product, put some of the money back into yourself. People like to see growth in their favorite artist or group.

If I buy a cd from you and the next cd look like you rushed through it, guess what I don't want it. There are too many artists that are willing to sacrifice time and energy into their project for you to just be comfortable at being average.

Understand your market and know what people want. Even though you want to be different, you still have to cater to your fans. We had another artist that would put posters up everywhere he goes, whether they take them down or not. Sometimes perception plays a big role in the industry as well; let people think of you as a star.

If people see something about you everywhere they go or they keep seeing your product in everyone's hands, they would want to know what's going on. It's just like hearing a song on the radio for the first time.

You may not like it but the more you hear it you'll begin to recite the words or eventually you'll end up liking the song.

That's what the radio wants you do. That's why they keep a song in rotation for so long. That's how we need to be in order to create a fan base. That's where perception comes into play. You may think an artist signed a major deal, but in reality he just organized a team to get his material out everywhere.

You don't have to make big moves all the time to make an impact on your career. The little steps count as well, like getting the proper promotional gear and spreading the word about your product or your movement.

Many people get into this industry thinking that it's easy to promote because they have the best product. You have to prove it to people. Just because you're the best at your craft, without the proper promotion, who will know it?

Don't let arrogance exceed reality, if you do, you'll get a quick reality check.

Another point I'd like to make is: YOU MUST BE ABLE TO ACCEPT FAILURE BEFORE YOU CAN ACHIEVE SUCCESS! That sounds crazy but let me explain. In my promotion company we have seen success at its finest. We've also been kicked when failure came our way.

BUT WE KEPT MOVING and that's the key to success! When I first started, I was a little naive about promoting. I thought that a good product sold itself. In most cases it does, only when it becomes successful. Most promoters have problems with failure, which could lead to a number of things. When club owners stop having faith in you, your product will be removed. YOU HAVE TO KEEP IT MOVING. Most club owners understand that it's going to be slow starting off. If the owner sees that you have given up, he or she will give up. However, if they see that you've stepped up your promotion and look at your loss as a stepping stone, he or she will work with you.

One thing a club owner wants from a promoter is Longevity. Thanksgiving of 08, we came up with the idea to give away a $1000 to the top artist or group in a hip-hop competition. We started promoting early. We wanted to make sure everyone knew about this event. We put artists on the flyers so they could help. The night of the event came and at the beginning only a few people came.

So we gave it a little while longer and a few more people came. We started to get a little nervous, considering we had to pay the $1000 plus pay our staff (dj, host, and security). By any means necessary, the show must go on regardless if we had to go in our pockets to pay. Due to good promotion and a good name behind our company, WE PACKED THE CLUB! Everyone came a little later. Needless to say that was an excellent night.

The night went so well that the owners wanted us to do a weekly show, which we have been doing nonstop for over a year. They liked the fact that we were confident and that we didn't give up. Even when times were looking bad, instead of making excuses we made options. Establish your self well; you never know when something small can lead to something big. So remember that the next time you're faced with a crisis due to promoting. Also, establish a good reputable and honest name for yourself. Most of the time that's all a person will see is your name on flyers, posters or magazines.

I have known plenty of people who decided against something because they saw a name or logo on a flyer of a person they didn't like. Now granted, there's always going to be someone talking about you whether good or bad.

There's going to be someone that just doesn't like you or your business. That's something that's uncontrollable, but the one thing that they shouldn't say is that you're not an honest person.

Remember, as a promoter your purpose is to make people a fan of your product. You can't do this, when you're dishonest or your product is not presentable. As I stated before, perception is everything.

We did a show in spring of 09 at a very upscale club. In this situation the club owner provided everything for us, from the flyer to the dj. We got this opportunity because of our hard work promoting different venues.

So we were on easy street, all we had to do was what we do best, PROMOTE! We even gave away a $1000 that night as well. With everything paid for up front, we had to take the money that was made from the door. Once everything was paid (dj, flyers, $1000) then we were able to take home the rest. The night of the event, I was in Las Vegas. My brother-n- law, who is my business partner, ran the event. I told him to give me a call after the show was over.

During the time of the event, I was getting calls from many artists wondering where I was. They also were congratulating me on our night. Since the club was packed, I was thinking that I'm coming home to a nice amount of money.

No one has ever called me or congratulated me on a showcase before, so this was big for me until I talked to my partner. He said that the night was good but it wasn't as packed as the 1st and 2nd time we promoted there.

The money at the door went to paying everyone else like the host, dj, security, and the $1000 giveaway. We only had a little money left, so we put that up for future shows. The perception of the show was great, everyone had a good time and they thought that we just made a ton of money not knowing what actually took place. THAT'S HOW WE WANT TO BE VIEWED! Even though we didn't make the money we wanted to make.

DID WE ACTUALLY FAIL? Think about that, because in my opinion we didn't. So learn how to take the good with the bad. You should be like a walking billboard, every time you talk to someone. You should mention your product. Even as an artist, you must promote.

Most often, we leave everything up to our promoters or managers to take care of the promoting side. Remember, your promoter or manager isn't going to be everywhere you are.

While they're promoting in one area, you should be promoting somewhere else. Whenever I go out, I bring some type of promotional item with me. If you're the type that's shy, make people ask you about your product.

Wear a promotional shirt or put your advertisement on your vehicle with a contact number. You'll be surprised about how many calls you get from people who are simply curious.

People like to buy things that have been heavily promoted. They feel as if they're getting their moneys worth and believe it or not, countless of people see your potential and will support you for that reason alone.

I have known people to purchase something from someone and will never use the item or will give it away. I had a friend like that, so I asked him why would he purchase an item from someone and not use it.

He said, "That kid is out everyday selling his products, an even though I don't need it he makes the product seem like a must have item." I used to do telemarketing and I wasn't that good at it. One of my supervisors helped me out by role playing. He was the customer and I was the telemarketer.

We went through a simulated call and afterward he told me I was dry, tired, and it seemed like I wasn't confident in the product. One thing he told me that stuck in my mind, in which I still do till this day is to say something positive such as "I'm great" or "I'm having an excellent day" when someone asks how you are.

He said, "Watch the response that people give you because they're so used to hearing or saying "I'm ok or just trying to make it."

HE WAS RIGHT! That helped boost my telemarketing sales because people could hear that I was confident and cheerful in my voice. You should try this and notice the response people give, it's amazing.

We research our product to be ready for any questions people have about it. Like I said before, people can sense when you don't know about the product. One of the worst things you can do is to kick a promoter while he's down.

If a show is not packed out, don't ask them questions such as: Did you promote this show? Remember, a promoter's job is to tell people about his product, so they can come out to support.

A promoter cannot directly control how many people show up. If you kick a promoter while he or she is down, 9 times out of 10 they won't show any sign of feelings toward you. The promoter just wants you to come to the next event.

BUT HE OR SHE WILL REMEMBER YOU! Promoters know a lot of people in the industry; you'll never know when someone may inquire about you. So never burn your bridges. WHAT DO YOU THINK HE OR SHE WILL SAY WHEN SOMEONE ASKS ABOUT YOU? This leads to my second point, don't, EVER ARGUE WITH A PROMOTER, especially over something insignificant.

A lot of artists kill their career by doing this. A promoter knows a lot about an artist before they spend the money to get them. If you have a history of being late to shows, causing trouble, arguing, and you're in and out of jail, a promoter will pass you up.

Everyone wants to win, but the less drama is better. Matter of fact an artist that's serious in this game and has a manager shouldn't even come in contact with the promoter. His manager should be his mouthpiece.

Even if a promoter is not on the up and up, it's not your job to spread the news. Trust me; their job is the fastest to go in this industry. If people don't support you, more than likely you're finished. If you're a dirty promoter people will see it and won't support you. I have seen so many promoters come and go. It's not easy depending on people to support you to make a living.

If you're starting out as a promoter always be truthful. If you're going to give money away, do it even if you have to use your own money because the club wasn't packed.

Remember; when you're giving money to the winner at your event make sure you're fair. Never say someone with a big name is coming to your club, UNLESS IT'S TRUE. One of the oldest tricks in the books is to say that an A&R will be looking for talent at the club.

If true, than that's fine, but nowadays, so many people are raising questions about this. If I'm going to promote an A&R at the club, I will have them on the flyer, in my text, and on the internet. Also, I would provide the A&R's name and record label.

That way you can look up his or her info to know it's legitimate or to see if your music fits their needs. When he or she walks into the club, they would be announced and seen. I'm not going to tell you the day after, that an A&R was there with no proof.

That's just not right; I want to be as honest as I can. Remember, like I said the goal is to have people come back. The worst thing to do is to be known as a con-artist or a dirty promoter in a game where you thrive on people and their support.

Promotions are not made for everyone but a lot of people feel that they can do it. They see what's in front of them but don't see the work or politics behind it.

IF YOU'RE DOING THIS JUST FOR MONEY, YOU'RE NOT GOING TO LAST! Being a promoter is like having the key to the industry.

The money can come quick and is unlike any other job. You don't have to get signed to start receiving money or have an artist signed to make money. Get people involved when you promote so that they will promote for you in return.

Organize a street team to help you distribute flyers. One day I was tired from working two shifts and passing out flyers. I went to 3 different clubs that night, the last club I went to I was dead tired. This guy that was less fortunate than me asked for some spare change.

I told the guy I will give him ten dollars if he would put flyers on every car on the parking lot. Needless to say he was all too excited to do this. I watched him put flyers on every car. When he was done, I gave him the $10 for a job well done.

You have to involve people when you promote. Another thing that we would do is to put different artists and their info on our flyer. That's 5000 flyers every month with your picture and info on it.

They would pass out the flyers because they want people to see them perform as well as create exposure for that artist. Small business owners should think about that when they tell a promoter that he can't put flyers in their business.

Understand that everyone that has a product needs advertising. So check places where promotional gear is allowed.

Ask business owners if they would allow you to put flyers out. Don't just leave them there because chances are, the owner will throw them out and that's a waste of time and money. If they let you leave flyers or promotional gear, go back to the business to see if they properly displayed them.

It wouldn't hurt to stay there for a while to see if people are actually picking up the flyers. Target areas were you know people will buy your product or attend your show. Local owned clothing stores, convenience marts and gas station are excellent places to promote.

Stay away from corporate owned business like big name clothing stores, unless you know someone who works there. Make sure they're able to promote your product during their shift and won't let anyone throw the material out.

Posters are always a good promotional tool, mainly because of the perception. When people see posters they automatically think the person is larger than life. Again, know where to hang a poster.

A good spot is at bus stops, local owned businesses, recording studios, schools etc. Reach out to local TV and radio stations; sometimes they'll let you advertise for free if you put their logo on your promotional gear.

We have a local TV station in my hometown that has a show dedicated to promoting local businesses or people that stand out in their community. THE BEST PART ABOUT THIS STATION IS, IT'S FREE!

What can be better than that? Find out all of your resources and USE THEM! You never know what can be effective, especially if it's FREE. Every time I mention Facebook or Myspace, I have people saying they don't have time for that. Some people might even go as far as to say, I don't want people knowing my business.

THAT'S BECAUSE THEY'RE USING IT WRONG! I even have people degrading social websites, saying they have better things to do with their time.

This is a big pet peeve, because people don't understand the power of it. Many go on these sites to socialize or to meet back up with people. For me, this spells FREE ADVERTISEMENT.

All you have to do is sign up and add friends to let them know about your product. For the people that think of this as being shallow, WISE UP. This is a promoters dream. Social networks have taken over. It's getting to a point where people are using Facebook to take care of all of their advertisement needs. That's great because it's FREE! It's fine to socialize and to meet new people; however, why not use the full power of Facebook.

There have been successful shows promoted where the only way you're invited is through Facebook. If you're promoting or selling something you can your have fellow friends help you promote through their page as well. All it takes is a little effort. When we throw shows, we have flyers, send text messages, and we send out invites on

Facebook. Between the 5 of us we each have over 2000 friends. When we send an invite out we're covering a lot of ground. A lot of people may not pick up our flyers, but they'll get the invite. A lot of people phones may be off, so they're not receiving the text. But they'll get the invite on Facebook.

When you're promoting you have to cover all grounds (INTERNET, TEXTING AND FLYERS). You can't rely on just one or 2 to be effective. I know a lot of people that go on Facebook multiple times a day, so use this very powerful tool to your advantage.

Sell yourself on Facebook; people like to see videos etc. If you have a camera, record yourself or the product you're selling. One good thing about Facebook is that you can tag your video to other people's page.

Now they can't help but to see you or your product. Myspace and Youtube are a little different but still very effective.

Youtube is more for the visual aspect of what the person is doing. If you can direct people to your Youtube site, you can have a nice following.

Youtube also ranks your video by how many views you have. Myspace is geared toward the artist or musician, unlike Facebook which might have more people joining to socialize or to look up old friends. Myspace is an artist's dream because it keeps track of your views and you can add songs on your page as well. It also keeps track of the people that listen to your songs. There have been people that were signed to a major recording deal off of Myspace. Now A&R's can look on your Myspace and see your, bios, pictures, music, etc. With these powerful internet tools, all you have to do is put a little effort behind it and you'll be on your way.

Booking shows

Now that you've got the promoting aspect down, it's time to book your first show. Finding a good venue is very important. You have to estimate your capacity, meaning if you're throwing a party and you started promoting early you should get a good outcome.

If you feel that a lot of people are coming, don't settle for a small venue just to save money. Remember, if you promote right you should at the very least get your money back. It's also important to know the area where you want to have your event.

Make sure it's the right spot for the type of event you're having. People are territorial; they like to go to events in their area or a well known area. Also, you want to cater to everyone. If you feel your location is good most people will support.

For example, in my city the best location for events is downtown because of all the main attractions. You may get a better turnout where people can relate to you. Location is a big concern, especially for women.

People like to be in a safe place with a well lit parking lot. Like I said before, you have to cater to peoples needs. Even if you're promoting and someone tells you that they would like to come, but it's too far or they feel better in their neighborhood. If you know your venue is in a good place, MAKE NO EXCEPTIONS! Now if you're in an area where cars are frequently stolen or people are getting robbed, you may want to reconsider. Even if there are lots of fights, people will link that to your event and the club. Also, when people mention your name or the club, they are going to pass on your event.

A few years ago a particular club; which was located in a questionable area had a lot of cars broken into and stolen; which prompted people to stop frequenting that club. Even though they weren't stealing the cars from the club lot, they were stealing the cars off of the streets when the lot was full.

That club took a bad rap, so they had to have security monitor the area so people can feel secure. Also, try to find a venue off of the highway or close to a major highway. I know people have GPS, but many don't.

If you're having out of town guests, this is important for them. We have held events in different locations and I have literally stayed on the phone inside of the club with the loud music playing trying to guide people to our venue.

Age limit is an important factor as well. Owners don't like to have people in their club who are underage. Club owners make their money off of the bar and a lot of times people under 21 like to fight or simply aren't able to purchase the bar; which is what the owners bank on.

A lot of club owners are starting to raise the age limit of their establishments because of that reason. If you're thinking about having an event that caters to 21 and younger you might want to look into a hall or an auditorium.

A CLUB OWNER'S LIQUOR LICENSE IS THEIR LIFELINE. Without it he's out of business, so he's not going to allow anyone to be the cause of him losing his liquor license. Now that you have your venue you have to get security if the club doesn't provide it for you. Most often the club owner adds security in the rental fee for your night. I know of one club owner that will not let you rent his establishment without at least 2 police officers at the event.

If you have to provide your own security, DON'T BE CHEAP! Get enough manpower to control the crowd. Again, DON'T BE CHEAP in order to save money.

Bouncing is a lot different than fighting; trust me I used to be a bouncer. You want to ensure everyone's safety as well as yours. You don't want anyone damaging the club or hurting your patrons. It might be a good ideal to hire police officers as well.

Their presence may deter people from fighting, because they can go to jail. Once you find a club you have to deal with the club owner.

Get to know them, find out if he's there just to make money or if he's an established businessman. There are many types of club owners, most of them were promoters who saved up enough money to open a club, so they can relate to you. Some owners may have made a lot of money and then decided to open a club. Some simply inherited from their family or have a family owned club.

Nevertheless, I have dealt with them all. All club owners pretty much have the same goals, TO GENERATE PROFITS! If you can't make them money they don't need you.

If you do make them money you become their "Go to Guy." Club owners also have a vision on the type of night they should have as well. If they trust you, they'll do a lot for you in return. This could ultimately lead to you owning your own club or at the very least, establishing a lasting relationship.

This is a very risky game and you're depending on people to make everything come together. So make sure you're doing everything on your part to create a successful event.

You as the promoter should only be concerned about bringing people to the club. If you're just starting off, a lot of club owners want you to pay to rent the club for your night.

There are other ways to establish your night once the club owner sees that you're consistent. One of the most popular ways to run your night is to agree upon the club owner having the bar and the promoter taking the door. You may have to promote there for awhile before this happens.

If the club owner knows of your events he may just split the door with you and you don't have to pay to rent the club. That's perfectly ok if you're starting off. If you're consistent and everything is going well, you should be able to negotiate to have the door money.

Remember, the club owner most likely will always have the bar and the bar will make the most money. So think about that if you have been promoting in a place for a while and the club owner is taking a percentage off of the door and has the bar. Build up a good relationship with the club owner. One of the clubs we have been promoting with finally paid off.

Originally, we were paying to rent the club but the door was always ours. After about 6 months of promoting with a successful show, we negotiated with the owner. He was willing to stop charging us to pay for the club.

That comes from us being consistent and the bar making good money. That makes a club owner happy and possibly wanting to invest in you and keep you around. Owners also like to hear of future plans. However, everyone else in town throwing the same type of events can cause their interest to subside. We had to switch up, because other promoters started doing the same things we were doing.

We noticed a decrease in numbers, so instead of standing by and waiting for the night to fade out, we came up with bigger and better ideas. It got to a point where the club owner was wandering what was going on because he seen

an increase of sales at his bar. YOU HAVE TO DO
WHAT YOU HAVE TO DO, just to stay afloat sometimes.
YOU HAVE TO PROMOTE. Once you involve the club
there are a lot of expenses that come into play. When
booking a show make sure you choose good dates.

Depending on the show, you want to pick the right dates.
For examples, Friday and Saturday are usually major club
nights because of the weekend, so if you're starting off you
may not want to book shows on those days.

But this shouldn't discourage you. Once you secure your
night, the promoting should begin. If you have a good
show lined up it shouldn't matter what day it's on. There's
always competition and some people like going to things
they are familiar with or have a close proximity to.

If you know that Wednesday is a night that everyone
frequents club XYZ which is centrally located, then you
may want to choose a different night. You don't have to
COMPETE, just be confident and determined.

AND NEVER GIVE UP! You have to start from
somewhere. It's very hard to draw a crowd to something
new on the same night as a previously established club or
event.

For instance, in my hometown we had a promoter that
came up with Martini Monday. On Monday's Martini's
were discounted along with other things as well. If I like
Martini's, guess what I'm there!

When you secure a date make sure you give yourself ample enough time to promote. If you choose a date 2 weeks from now and your flyers won't be back till next week, you probably should have given yourself a month to promote.

Remember, this is your TIME, MONEY AND EFFORT ON THE LINE, so making good decisions is necessary. Don't choose a date for your event because you need some quick money on that day.

So stay on your P's and Q's or you may find yourself in a bad situation. For example, one night about a couple of years ago, this artist wanted us to check his group out because they wanted us to manage them.

He said that they were opening up for this major artist. He gave us free tickets to the event, so we went. We're always looking for new connections. Now my ears are always in the streets and my eyes are always glued to the internet to see what's going on.

No one heard about this event that we were going to, but I didn't think anything about it. We arrived early and the club was empty which didn't strike us as odd since people generally come out much later. We started networking and we found the promoter that threw the show.

As time went on, there wasn't any sign of the major artist. So we talked to the promoter to see what was going on. He said that the major artist and his entourage had trouble finding the club. By this time the club was on its last hour before closing with no sign of the major act. The promoter (a non local) was almost in tears. The club had about 20 people total and he said that he had given the major act manager half of the money up front with no contract.

I'm not going to tell you the amount because it's utterly embarrassing as a promoter myself to conduct business like this with NO CONTRACT! So we'll just say it was a very nice amount of money. When he told me that, I felt bad for him since he had obviously been taken advantage of. To make matters even worse, the promoter had brought more people with him from out of town than the amount of people who showed up at the club locally.

Needless to say, the money he spent to bring down the major act was gone. He also had to pay the club, plus the dj and sound man. We called some artist for him to come and perform and he just turned the night into an open mic session (a very expensive open mic session might I add). Now let's recap, some of the issues that went wrong that night.

First off, when you're promoting out of town you must do your homework. He had it on a Friday night which is a strong club night and it was during the Gateway Classic weekend. There was a lot going on that weekend. Now usually when you bring down a major act you can get away with booking a show on an eventful weekend, however, his major act wasn't strong enough to get people to come just by word of mouth.

With a very popular major act, you can pretty much make a successful night just by saying his/her name. Even if you went that route you still want to have heavy promotion as well. It should have been promoted a great deal. I didn't see any flyers out on the streets except on the night of the club. I didn't hear people talking about it. He needed a local street team to help promote while he was out of town.

And last but certainly not least, you should ALWAYS conduct business with a CONTRACT! They took his money and there was nothing he could do about it. Like I said before, no one can be trusted in this industry, especially when money is involved.

That night could have been an excellent night with the proper promoting techniques. If you ever feel that you don't understand something, by all means talk to a lawyer and ask lots of questions.

Or at least talk to someone with a lot of experience. In this game WHAT YOU DON'T KNOW CAN HURT YOU! Sometimes dealing with the artist and manager is ok. When you have to deal with the entourage it makes your experience with that artist different and oftentimes difficult.

Entourages are the artist's support team and for the most part are there just for the artist. Sometimes the entourage can kill an artist's career, before the artist has made it in the industry. Once you make it, it's different for the artist; he has more responsibilities, an image to maintain, and more deadlines to meet. Many times his crew doesn't understand the transition from the streets to the industry. So they feel that the artist doesn't want to hang with them anymore or doesn't have time for them. You can't continue living and doing the same things that you were doing before the deal. The label has invested money in you and they don't want to see their investment in jail or dead.

If your entourage is doing the things you used to do, you now have to stay away from that and focus on your craft while maintaining a professional demeanor at all times. As an artist, the worst thing you can be labeled as is an artist that causes trouble.

You're a promoter and a club owner's worst enemy and a huge liability. During my bouncing days, every time this certain artist came in the club we knew a fight was going to occur, primarily because of his associates being out of control.

A promoter or club owner wants to protect their investment so they don't want you to come in and tear up their place. We all know that sometimes, artists make their money mostly from shows rather than record sells.

So if you're labeled as a troublemaker, no one will want to deal with you. If you have to distance yourself from your entourage, SO BE IT! You're in this industry to achieve success. If your entourage can't see the importance of your status, then they can care less about your dreams. If they're your true friends then they'll understand and be on your side. Now you're in a position to help people and you're making the kind of money that can change a person's lifestyle. You're at the top and your friends are at the bottom. They're looking at you as a savior.

You've worked hard to achieve your success so the last thing you want to do is be frivolous with money and start giving it away. SO WHAT DO YOU DO? YOU GIVE YOUR FRIENDS JOBS! Sounds good, right?

To have people handling your fan mail and internet promotions and to have your 6 foot 5 friend be your bodyguard is great! You can do this now! It works, if they really are serious about helping you, but if they're lazy and you know it, don't even considering employing them.

Make them earn it. Remember, the people under you represent you. If anything happens good or bad, people are automatically linking you with it. Be careful who you give jobs to because you are always under scrutiny.

Meaning, you never know what the money you give them is used for. The worst case scenario is that you're in the middle of a FBI case and you have no idea what's going on, but they linked you because your money was used to fund something illegal.

That goes for anybody you deal with not just friends. Do your background checks on people. Remember, you're in the limelight and everyone else would like to be in your position as well.

So they'll do what it takes to get theirs. Also, if someone gets into trouble, chances are they won't hesitate to drop your name in their situation just to bring you down. YOUR FAME AND MONEY WILL GAIN FRIENDS, BUT WILL GAIN MORE ENEMIES!

Everybody is looking forward to a good show and you're excited to see how many people are going to show up. Your promotion was good, but the one thing that can ruin a show is sound. I never knew how important this was until about 3 years ago.

We used to hear so many complaints about the sound system at the club where we were promoting. People actually stopped coming to our shows because of the poor sound quality. It's important that you have a good sound man with all the equipment needed to run the show.

The club might not have certain things that you need i.e. a cordless mic. Depending on the type of show you may want to have your host mobile so that he/she is able to mingle with the crowd. Most clubs don't have a cordless mic or if they do, it's used for special occasions only.

But a good sound man will have one. He should have a good mobile sound system. What if you rented a hall with no system? That's where the sound man comes in. Most sound men are dj's as well, so you have a package deal. He must be reliable and should be the first person on site along with you, just in case the artists want to do sound checks prior to the show starting.

He must know how to operate the equipment at all times. Remember the dj and sound men have different jobs. Without the sound man the dj is useless. A dj is there to plug his equipment into the sound system. The sound man is there to make sure it's being hooked up properly and the sound is good.

Last year we were promoting for a club and we had a show/party. Our dj arrived early but there was no sound man. For hours, there wasn't any music, so we finally got in touched with the owner. He said that everything was set up and ready to go.

He didn't want to pay for his sound man to come out. He also said, "The dj should know where to plug into." BUT, HE WAS WRONG! That was our dj's first time at that club and he didn't want to be liable for any damages.

Equipment is expensive. The setting could be set for a different type of show. That's why you need a sound man there to make adjustments. Sometimes you have to spend a little money to ensure that you won't have to spend big money to replace broken equipment.

Let the sound man be accountable for the sound, after all, that's his expertise. You want people to have a good time at your establishment, which includes but is not limited to having crystal clear sound. Artists like to have their music loud and precise when they perform as well. People will decide if they want to buy your cd based on your performance.

So if your performance doesn't sound good due to the sound system, no one is going to buy your cd. Everyone loves a good show and more important the promoter loves putting on a good show.

Every promoter is going to face having a bad night. It may be due to a small crowd because of another venue having a good night, or maybe you expected more money, but you realized you let a lot of people in free.

WHAT DO YOU DO? Never let them see you sweat, like I said before, perception is everything to a promoter. Act like the night was a good night in front of your guest. Don't make excuses, it is what it is.

There is nothing worse than the promoter making excuses about why the night is slow. I'm here to support you, things happen. You can't make people come out, the only thing you can do is give them a reason to come out.

Re-think your night; find out why it didn't go as planned. This is not the time to back down or feel sorry for yourself. It's time to promote better, network harder, and pass out all your flyers, especially if this is your first event.

Sometimes a bad night is a reality check. If you had so much success in the past you might have slowed down a bit on the promoting. Or you might not have ordered as many flyers or relied on others to spread the word. So when you have a bad night, that's your wake up call. It will bring you back to realty.

Every night is not destined for success. YOU HAVE TO PUT IN WORK! There might be many more bad nights or this might be your only one. Nevertheless, you must know how to deal with it. We have had plenty of bad nights but or guests couldn't tell. They may even commend you on your night.

If you carry yourself successfully people are going to think you're prosperous. Club owners see your glory as well as your downfalls. They want a promoter that's going to handle the good and deal with the bad.

PROMOTERS ARE VERY REPLACEABLE! So think of your bad nights as an example of what not to do. Now you have a guideline of how to run your event.

Your Staff

Everybody has dreams and would like to execute them to the fullest potential, HOWEVER, YOU CANNOT DO THIS ALONE! You need people that will help you fulfill your dreams. When you assemble your team, keep in mind that any help is good help.

Meaning, some people may not have the same passion as you, so their work ethic may not be as strong as yours. Don't push that person away especially if they're helping out. Oftentimes, you must be a mentor as well as a leader.

So lead by example instead of by word. When I first started, I was taught things that I still do to this day. People must believe in you so you must have discipline.

Remember to help other people with their dreams as well. Don't just pick people because they're your friends or relatives. That can cause a lot of problems in your company. Don't just hire a person because they talk a good game.

We had a couple people work with us and they realized this was a serious commitment; this is like a second job. Some people left and some stayed. As for me, I never missed a beat. In order to excel in this industry you must stay focused. Just because you work hard for a period of time doesn't mean you'll be established in this business. I think that a lot of people forget their purpose after a while. Then they feel like people owe them something for their small impact in music. I've seen this happen to promoters, managers, artist etc. They start off working hard but after a while if they're not seeing the results they want to see then they'll slack off. There are NO GUARANTEE'S IN THIS INDUSTRY!

You must have people that are willing to go the distance with you. I love it when people who I haven't seen in a while come to a show and say, "You're still doing your thang." I might respond by saying, "We never stopped."

As your success level starts to rise, people who didn't deal with you before all of a sudden witness your growth and potential. Now they want a piece of the pie. They might come to you offering to do shows with you or to put their money in for a large payout.

You must decide if they're an investor, a promoter or simply in it for the GREEN! Anybody can throw their money in offering to help but will it cause problems? We ventured with another company to do a show and decided we would split the door after everyone was paid.

He came to us saying he has a huge following on social networking sites and we had the host, club, and a dj. So we gave him a chance. We did our thing, promoting on the streets and on the internet. We didn't really see him that much, but he said he was promoting. The night of the show was ok, there weren't a lot of his followers there but it was a decent amount of people who showed up. At the end of the show we started counting the money.

We made a nice amount, so he started to get happy. He stated that he wanted to do this monthly, maybe even weekly if it starts getting crowded. This is how a lot of new promoters feel when their first show goes as planed. Until we started taking money out to pay people like the club, dj, and the host. He then got upset, saying he could have gotten a host and dj for free, but he came to us and that's how we ran our show.

We didn't complain having to give a portion of our money away. Like I said before, just because people have money or a good idea doesn't mean they're easy to work with especially if they're interfering with the way your shows are run.

That's a distraction and can ruin a good company as well as business relationship. KNOW THE PEOPLE YOU WORK WITH! It makes it easier in the long run. Watch out for people that just want to make money and really don't have a passion for the business.

There's nothing better than to walk in a place and be greeted by a beautiful woman. Having women on your staff is necessary. I have seen guys change their mind about coming into a club just by talking to the girl at the door. Women attract other women as well as men.

We used to take turns taking the money at the door, until we hired a woman to assist us. We noticed that more women were coming to the club which attracted the guys. Now our club scene stayed consistent with the number of people we wanted to have. On flyers, people use women to promote their event to make people come out. Women can make things happen or get you into places you thought you couldn't get into. Ever since we hired our assistant, we noticed more people reaching out to us.

There's something about a woman that makes promoters or club owners feel that she has to be a part of the event. Or it takes a woman's touch to make a normal event more elegant and appealing to others. We were networking with people we thought we would never be able to network with.

Whether you have women models, a woman working the door, or hosting, simply having them as a part of the team has its advantages. Sometimes women are more dedicated than men, because they want to prove a point or they have large support groups.

Just make sure you hire a woman who's dedicated and understands that this is a business. On the other hand women can cause problems in your establishment. They can be emotional or sometimes be easily distracted.

We have had women work for us before and it didn't work out for us or them. We had a lady work for us in the past and she dated one of the artists that came to our show. It was great when they were together, but when they broke up he stopped coming as well as his group. That's 8 people that stopped coming to our show because of a relationship. That's a prime example of mixing business with pleasure. This is your company and everybody you hire represents you and the company. People will rate your company off of your employees, so if you have someone that's not trustworthy, that can bring your accountability down. Finding good help is hard, but bad help comes easily.

Stay away from people wanting you to hire them because they feel that the company is doing well, so they want to be in the spotlight. Try to find someone that loves the business and has good work ethics. This will make your company grow. Everyone wants to make money and everyone has good ideas, but everyone is not trustworthy. Being a promoter in some cases come with a lot of power.

You control the show, you're the one bringing the money in and you're the one everyone wants to know. When you hire new people give them a sort of probationary period, especially when it comes to money.

MONEY CHANGES PEOPLE, especially large amounts. It can turn families and friends against one another. Some people can't deal with money without thinking wrong ideas. In this industry trust goes a long way but can easily be broken. We have been called a lot of names, but one name you can't call us is dirty.

We have walked out after our shows with nothing because we gave prize money to the artist and had to pay our staff. Now you may not believe it, just do the math.

NUMBERS DONT LIE! We would rather have a successful show and the money will come. You can't just

41

focus on making the money because you might be a one hit wonder in this industry. Never lie about an event and never defraud your workers of their earnings.

If you say someone is headlining and people paid to see this than DELIVER YOUR PROMISE! Don't get labeled as unreliable, that's the quickest way to go out of business. Sometimes it may take a while for your event to do well, but hang in there.

Don't lie about things to have people come to your event, it only makes things worst. Have integrity about your event and people will respect you. DON'T FALL VICTIM TO THIS, just to make a couple of extra dollars. Remember, you might not say anything but people talk. A couple of years ago, we did a showcase series at this well know club.

We did extremely well that night. A lot of people performed and had a good time. We did a follow up show a couple of months later due to the success of the first show. Some people didn't get a chance to perform on the first show because they got there too late.

So people arrived early for this show to make sure they had a performance slot. This one guy came to the second show because he heard of the success of the first show. But he came late and wanted to have his artist perform.

He was on the standby list but judging by the amount of people, he wasn't going to be able to perform. So he really wanted to get on the first list.

We had media at the show and some celebrities. You can understand why he wanted to get on the list.

So he placed a large sum of money in my hand and asked me "When can my artist perform?" I gave the money back and told him we don't do business like that. Now I could have taken the money and told our host to put him up next.

I had the power to do that and I could have pocketed the money, but here is where integrity, honesty and trust come into play.

You don't know how many people would have seen me do that and now he knows that I can be brought. Anytime someone wants to excel on the list just go to me with some money.

That's not fair to the other people that paid their money to get in that got there early. I told some people about that and they said I was crazy for not excepting the money because I had the power to do that.

But I would rather run the show right than to make a couple of extra dollars and ruin my brand. We also made a nice amount of money the RIGHT way. That's one of the reasons why we have one of the longest running showcases in St. Louis.

When you pick your elite staff, remember that a job title is just a title. Make sure your staff doesn't let their title go to their head by using their power the wrong way. If you hire someone as your vice president, they should take it seriously and should be your right hand person. They should know the business just as well as you do. They should be a good leader and not drunken with power. He or she should be a good decision maker.

If our company travels a lot and one day the owner can't make it, the vice president should take over and everything should run just as smoothly. You should have just as many if not more contacts.

People should respect you not for the position that you're in but by your work ethics. Like I said before a person will not work harder than you for a goal that will uplift your name, however they will work equally as hard if they see that you are. People should know who you are. Meaning, they should associate you with the company. People should know to talk to you if they can't get the CEO.

This is something that you earn through time. By being professional, knowing the business, and going to all of the events. People will automatically know who's in charge by your actions and your demeanor. When I first started, no one knew me until I started networking with people.

My name was being referred to the company. I didn't have to tell people I was the president or second in command, they automatically assumed that. That didn't happen over night; I just put myself in the right places and conducted myself accordingly. The host is the attention getter.

You must have an excellent speaking voice and always know what's going on with the company. You must also have a good relationship with the dj. Our host and dj use signals to communicate when they're not next to each other. A good host knows people and their status.

One thing that people like when they come to an event is to get recognition when they walk in. You also must be able to get the message out to the crowd. In most cases the host is the crowd control.

When we did a show at this club for the first time, the club owner kept telling me that our host was really good and that he controlled the crowd well. If you're really good you can name your fee and most promoters don't mind paying.

This is a good way to get your feet wet in the business, especially if you have an excellent speaking voice. An assistant is very crucial in this industry. They're the brains for your successful company.

He or she must have excellent bookkeeping skills. This person should be able to go out a lot and network with people. Their public relations skills and image should be excellent as well.

Every time this person is out or talking to people they represent your company. They must be trustworthy and universal; must be able to run the show as well. We had a number of assistants, they would start off good but after a while they would slack off. Eventually they would quit. In the industry you must give a hundred percent at all times. We just hired our current assistant about six months ago and she gives 100% at all times to complete a task.

She listens and wanted to excel in this industry. Every time she goes out she represents our name in a good way. That's what any company needs to be successful. In the past we would try people out without pay and after a while they would complain.

But you have to earn your pay. With our assistant now, she was willing to work with no pay to prove that she was worthy to be on the payroll. It didn't take her long to get there. If you're looking to become an assistant, learn everything you need to know about the company.

It will only help you in the long run. Your street team is important because they're advertising your product. ANYBODY CAN BE A PART OF THE STREET TEAM.

They are the one's who're putting flyers on cars, have some type of promotional gear on, or hanging up posters. A lot of companies fail at conquering this market by not having a strong street team or not having a street team at all.

You must have a trustworthy team that you know will pass out the advertisement of your product and not throw it away. Remember, until your company grosses millions, YOU ARE A PART OF YOUR STREET TEAM!

There's no one that you can trust better than yourself. People used to be amazed to see me or the CEO passing out flyers or actually answer our phones. They felt that we should have people under us to do this.

But we're not Hollywood, we realize the fact that we can't depend on anybody to do this for us. When you have an event, you need to conquer every aspect of promoting. So if that means you have to pass out flyers in the snow, rain, or sleet, SO BE IT.

Your hard work will pay off. Our head street team guy will go to the extreme to pass out our promotional gear. Whether day or night, we can depend on him. He's so good that other companies wanted to pay him for passing out their promotional gear as well.

Assembling the right street team is very important. They're the one's that make your product visible to the world. Those are the type of people you need to survive. Like I said before, anybody can be on the street team, but be careful with your family and friends.

This is your business, but some people don't treat it that way. Most of the times when you're starting off a lot of these jobs are without pay. It's important to select your staff wisely. People are willing to work for free, if they share the same dream as you.

For example, if a person can see the company growing into an empire, they wouldn't mind working hard to see that day. Sometimes family members mix business with pleasure or make business personal. That's not going to work; you can't give everyone a job. Some people don't have good work ethics. Sometimes jealousy comes into play. Everyone can't be the boss.

Everyone must have a role. In this business there are a lot of women that attend this type of event. You must have a staff that is not easily distracted. If one of your staff members are watching the money at the door and a pretty lady walk through, his attention is on her.

WHO'S WATCHING THE MONEY! That's a good set up to be robbed. When it comes to money your focus and attention should be on that. People are desperate and will do anything to get your mind off the money.

So be careful and put someone who is responsible at the door to handle the money. At my event I don't like to drink, I may have one drink that night but that's my limit. This is very important; when someone is intoxicated it's very hard to run a successful operation.

When a person is drunk you don't know what's going to happen and you can't maintain a sense of control. I had a friend that used to curse out women when he got drunk. That's bad business to hire someone like him, he would run everyone out.

It's ok to have a good time, but your focus should be having a successful drama free night. You want your night to be a respected night. And all it takes is one mess up to ruin your event. Also, fighting is a good way of being put out of business as well. Surround yourself with good level minded people. Stay away from people that seem to always find themselves in trouble, especially in your establishment.

People don't think about how much you can lose by fighting and damaging the place. That doesn't sit well with the club owners even though it wasn't your fault, it was your event. Be smart when selecting your staff, because they represent you.

You might risk hurting people's feelings, but trust me, if you know that they won't work out, don't even waste your time.

I know that family is important but there is a very thin line between family and business and if you cross that line the results can be very catastrophic. Now your staff is pretty much complete. Everyone is doing their job and your company is doing well, but what about those miscellaneous duties that need to be taken care of?

Managing artists, you'll find that they have certain needs, like cd duplication or artwork. Remember every cd or merchandise that the artist has represents you. So it must be good and well organized.

So get to know a graphic designer or someone to duplicate cd's. The worst thing to have is an artist with your company name on their cd with no type of label or graphics work. You want to stand out in this industry by being more professionally represented. Lack thereof could result in you missing out on the big ticket. Also, have someone design your Myspace page or website. Sometimes the first place a person will look you up is on your web page or your Myspace page.

If you have good graphics, up to date info, and a lot of hits on your page, people will take you serious and would want to do business with you. I get a lot of compliments on my Myspace page, because of the info about shows and artists.

Increase the number of friends and the amount of views on your site. The more people talk about your event the more people will come out. Also, create a company page and have someone dedicated to working that page as well.

Don't slack up on Myspace or any other social site, people have been discovered and people sell their music as well as their beats. If it's used for the right purpose, these social networking websites are very useful.

The internet is a powerful tool if you use it right. Sometimes your page can make you look like a star before anyone gets the chance to meet you. Like I said before and I'm going to keep saying it. PERCEPTION IS EVERYTHING IN THIS INDUSTRY!

You also want an in-house or a person you can count on to videotape. Video is very important; it allows people to see your events when they can't physically attend them. Make sure they can edit and can also post videos in a timely manner. I do our videos for the company and it makes it convenient for us because I'm a part of the team and I always go out of town as well. Our artist did an out of town show in this small town. They opened up for a major artist, so the club was packed.

I got good footage of the performance as well as the crowd. I posted on the internet and a lot of people commented on the performances. Now people want to go there and perform or see what the town is about because our artists look like stars based on the video footage.

That's the power of video; I bring the energy and excitement to the viewers. If you're preparing for an event do a commercial or trailer for it to get people interested. People like to see people having a good time.

Now we shoot a commercial for every event we do. It's quick and easy and it's really a good way to promote to people who've never attended your events. You want to have a staff that can understand your vision.

Like I said before when you're starting off you might not have the budget to pay your staff. If they're willing to stay with you during the tough times then as you grow, they'll definitely be there during the good times.

With hard work and proficient work ethics your company will be successful. Don't let anyone take that away from you. Working together to accomplish a common goal is what any company needs, especially starting off. Victory is only just one show or event away. Just focus on the business and everything else will fall in place.

Proper Etiquette

I'm an artist, a manager and a promoter. I've been doing this for a while. The one thing I've noticed from this business is the LACK OF BUSINESS. We as artists, promoters, and record labels are pros when it comes to our craft.

Honestly that's just 30% of this industry, mainly because of everyone else trying to get in the industry. We are lacking when it comes to the business aspect. One of my artists will tell anyone who talks to him directly in this industry to speak to his manager.

He feels that he might say something that will ruin a deal. That's being smart because your manager is your mouthpiece and you as an artist should stick to your craft. But not everyone has a manager to speak for them.

There is a rapper born everyday. That's understandable, but a lot of times rappers don't realize that they can damage their career by opening their mouths. You may think that you're the hottest rapper, prove it instead of telling the dj's.

For me, I love it when one of my songs play and people ask "Who is this?" and I'll reply, "Me" and they'll say, "I didn't know you rap this is a great song."

They'll tell the wrong people things they wouldn't do instead of the things they should do. The funny thing about it is that the same people complaining HAVEN'T SOLD

ONE RECORD! That's what it's all about SELLING RECORDS IN THIS INDUSTRY! Learn the game before you play. Otherwise, you'll be the center of the joke and people won't take you serious. This industry is roughly 70% business and 30% music.

It doesn't matter if your business isn't right. Just because you have a manager doesn't mean that you're next to being signed. Do the research on the industry, what you don't know CAN HURT YOU.

Sometimes a manager can hurt your career if they don't know what they're doing. Learn to be a one man team; there is no one that will uplift you more than yourself. Instead of depending on others provide for you.

Information is out there, you just have to grab it. We say that we work hard in this industry to make it, but actually we take this for granted. Instead of selling our products we'll give up if a couple of people don't buy it.

Then we resort to our old way of living. We believe everything that people say. Anybody that does numbers in this industry would tell you it's a business first then music.

Let's think business first, let's find out how to market ourselves and our products.

Let's have the labels bidding on us, instead of us chasing them and having them close the door in our faces. Let's support each other by giving honest opinions about our product so we can give the labels good music. Let's be more consistent on our product instead of just release an album or mixtape one every 5 years. If this is your life or if this is how you survive you have to stay busy.

Let's understand how things work before we just dive in head first. Trust me on this one, HIP-HOP IS NOT DEAD, IT'S JUST WAITING ON YOU TO GET YOUR BUSINESS RIGHT!

Being a promoter and manager, I get a lot of calls from artists wanting to get into shows or wanting management or promotions. I know that being young is golden in this industry or that slang is a part of our culture.

BUT PEOPLE YOU ARE HURTING YOURSELVES BY NOT KNOWING HOW TO SPEAK TO PEOPLE. I get phone calls daily from artists talking to me like we're on the streets.

You don't know who I am. Not to say I have a big name, but if you talk that way to me, who knows who else you're talking to. I have a few pet peeves about this. I can be the connection you need to make it in this industry.

But you'll never know because you're not serious. When you're asking about shows or calling for management you should be professional or have someone talk for you. If you're not serious, the person on the other side won't take you serious. Leave all the slang and tough talk for your music.

When you're off the stage that's when your business mind should take place. There's a big misconception about major artist or established independent artist. A lot of unsigned artist think that the way they talk in their music is the way to conduct business. This is false. Your image sells records but your knowledge makes you money.

PERCEPTION IS EVERYTHING! A major successful artist doesn't go around shooting people or selling drugs. They probably did before the major deal, but now they're worth money so they have to carry themselves in a professional manner.

AND SO SHOULD YOU. When you talk to someone, you never know, they could be in a position to advance your career. You don't have to convince them that you're the greatest thing to music. TRUST ME, THEY WON'T BELIEVE YOU.

Your actions will always speak louder than your words. What if the person doesn't like your material and you spent all that time trying to persuade them that you're the best? You're just wasting time and energy.

You should be humble at all stages of your career, especially at the beginning. Sometimes people want to help but your attitude is so bad that they don't want to deal with you. I hear so much about people complaining and that they deserve to be on, but 6 months later they're not even doing music anymore. We have a show every Thursdays and I understand that artists can't make every show, but don't down talk a showcase because you feel that you're too important, or bigger than life. Until you sell records you can't afford to talk down on anything. If you don't want to come out, don't come.

Don't make excuses about the show. We're for our city, to expose the artist in our city. Contrary to popular belief, we show love to all independent artists.

Everyone wants to get a chance to shine and in most cases this is the only way for most rappers to do so. Your words go a long way in this industry.

Remember, I'M NOT THE ENEMY; I'm here to help you make a name for yourself. The rap game is hard, SO DON'T MAKE IT HARDER! You may think that you're being real or keeping it one hundred but sometimes you need to know when to keep your mouth closed.

I get occasional phone calls from artists and they're complaining about other promoters, club owners or radio dj's.

You don't know who I am friends with nor do business with. Who do you think a major label A&R is going to ask about you? Those same promoters, club owners, or dj's that you just spoke badly about. Now you just ruined a good business opportunity for yourself.

As an artist, I know that we take our music serious. So if someone pisses you off, you feel the need to retaliate.

DON'T! Don't even think about recording a diss song aimed at a promoter or dj. For one, you shouldn't show your anger. Secondly, most promoters or djs are not rappers so your diss song is irrelevant. Like I mentioned before, you don't know who the promoter or dj knows that can take your career a step higher.

BE A MAN OR WOMAN and sit down and talk to that person that pissed you off (9 times out of 10 it was a misunderstanding). What if the person didn't know you were mad at him, maybe it's something that can be easily fixed, but you have to give them a chance.

You're living your life with a grudge and that person doesn't have a clue. I don't know how many times someone got pissed off at our shows and was mad and waited until something else happened to tell us.

We would easily fix the problem if necessary. We had an artist not to long ago complain about our show. Instead of asking who put on the show he decided to pick up a flyer and text the first number he saw, which was me.

In his text he cussed at our host, the club, judges and at our company. The sad thing was that he didn't know who he was texting. THIS IS LIKE SUICIDE FOR YOUR CAREER! So I decided to call this artist back and have a one on one with him.

He was upset because he felt that he should have won. So he said that the Judges cheated. This phone call lasted about 2 hours, early in the morning. I explained to him that you should never show your anger or send a nasty text to someone you don't even know

I could have taken this the wrong way and could have been after him but there was no need for that. So finally we came to an agreement. I told him let's sit down and talk at the showcase next week and I'll get you in free. As a promoter/manager I like to handle situations as professionally as possible.

So the following week he came to our show and I walked up to him, he didn't know who I was. We introduced ourselves he gave me a handshake as if we were best friends. At that point I know that he wasn't a confrontational type of person.

In this industry, sometimes it takes the bigger man to solve a problem. So I asked him very politely, what was with all the hostility last week.
HE SAID THOSE FAMOUS WORDS THAT I LOVE TO HEAR PEOPLE SAY WHEN THEY'RE CONFRONTED:

"I was drunk when I talked to you last week; you have to excuse my behavior." If I was someone important that could have helped his career, he would have ruined any chances he had due to being inebriated.

Believe it or not we're not the enemy and we also GET MAD. But we're supposed to be professional; I just wish that everyone else would be.

Instead of lashing out your anger take a minute and think about the situation. Put yourself in our shoes, WHAT DO WE HAVE TO GAIN BY SCREWING YOU! Then you'll understand that this is a business. Just because you know the promoter, THIS IS STILL A BUSINESS and we can't please everyone.

We get complaints about artists not being able to perform when they showed up late, or complaints about things that we had no clue about what happened or something that didn't even involve us.

For example, every Thursday we have a show where we give away $200 to the top artist or group. We also have different judges every week. A couple of weeks ago we had an artist that came in that hasn't been to our shows in a while.

The artist had a complaint about one of our shows last year. The judges didn't judge that artist because we had "not paid" by the artist name on the sign up sheet. We used to allow artist that we knew to sign up first then if they need to go home and change they can come back and pay to get in.

When the artist came back and paid the girl at the front door forgot to erase the "not paid" from his name. So when the host seen it, he told the judges not to judge that artist. Our rule was you have to pay at the door to compete for the $200. At the end of the night, the judges added up the score to see who won.

At that time we were picking 10 winners to go to the finals at the end of the month to compete for $500. The first place weekly winner will get $200.

When they didn't call that artists name for the top ten, he felt something was wrong. So the judges told the artist that they were instructed by the host not to judge him because of the "not paid" stamp by his name.

THIS WAS A HONEST MISTAKE; THE HOST WAS DOING HIS JOB! So the artist got really angry and said we cheated him and the voting was rigged. Now we didn't even know what was going on, but when we asked the judges they said the artist would have made the top ten if he would have been judged.

So we told the artist, he'd made it to the top 10 and we gave him his money back to be fair, but the artist was still mad and didn't want to hear what we had to say.

But we can't help that a mistake was made. So at least give us the courtesy of fixing the situation before it gets out of control. We weren't privy to what was going on but we took the blame for it and we tried to correct the problem.

Do you know that this person went on Facebook and spoke badly about us saying we were hating on him? We didn't even know about this incident till the end of the showcase. The artist also said we cheated him. BUT DOESN'T THAT SOUND LIKE THE ARTIST HATING ON US!

What angered me the most is that this artist won money from us, we put him in our magazine, on our flyers and radio commercials for FREE!

Now do you see what promoters have to go through? I guess it's true what they say, you can't please everyone. The show must go on. One person can't stop our show!

NOW, DO YOU STILL WANT TO BE A PROMOTER? SURE YOU DO. Promoting is fun you get to deal with artists that feel that they're the next BIG thing.

They don't mind telling you every chance they get But as stressful as that might be you have to honor or at least listen to what they're saying.

Remember, these artists feel that you're the answer to them making it in the industry. So they're going to give you their life story. If you want that artist to come to your show you have to listen to them. Your job should be to give them advice if you have been doing this for a while.

Be honest with them; let them know if they're doing something wrong. Some of these artists are very talented but don't have that professional support so they have to handle the business part with no help.

They may not know how to talk to people or how to take care of business for that matter, but as a promoter, you have to know how to handle people. This could determine how many people come through the doors for your event.

It can get stressful, but this is your job. I get a lot of calls, especially before a show. I try to answer every call, if I don't I will call back. I get compliments, for explaining our show in detail to every customer.

Just understand that people are excited when it comes to music. I give advice to people trying to become promoters, I don't hold back info, and I want everyone to be successful and to build strong network relationships.

I want to be able to live off of this industry. We need artists just as much as artists need promoters, so I give artists their due respect. If I have to answer 100 phone calls a day from artists talking about the same thing, I'll do it with no hesitation.

This is what builds your events. I had an artist tell me, "That's good that the person that is throwing the show is actually calling artists to come to the show." Now as an artist, whenever you network with people remember to have a business mind especially with promoters. Make sure you give them a CORRECT PHONE NUMBER or a number that is working.

I have received demos that I've liked from artists in clubs. One thing I like to do is call the artist to give him or her feedback or an invite to our show, but when I call the number, it's disconnected.

If this happens to me, imagine if they gave a cd to an A&R representative. They would have missed out on an opportunity. Who knows, you may only get 1 chance. Make sure you give out your personal number or if you don't have a personal number please provide your government name.

When I give you a call and your mother answers the phone, it's quite embarrassing when I have to ask for Killer tha Don of STL. Now your mother thinks I'm playing on the phone and curses me out because she doesn't know your alias.

Then you call a minute later apologizing. People this is the 21st century buy a cell phone or pay the bill. Also, when I call your number I don't want to listen to you freestyle or play an entire song before you answer the phone; especially when I'm trying to leave you a message.

LETS BE PROFESSIONAL! If you want me to listen to music, get a website, Facebook, or Myspace. When I call you, that's not the appropriate time to have me listen to your song on the phone.

That's the time to conduct business; anything else is a waste of time. There goes your opportunity once again. Make this as easy as possible. When you talk to people in the industry, keep in mind that they have some type of experience dealing with artists. If they ask you then you can tell them your list of accomplishments.

A lot of artists feel that they have to tell anybody of importance their musical life story. Remember, they listen to a lot of dreams, life stories, and lies, so stand out in their eyes. Also, your actions speak louder than words.

If you tell me how you have so many shows out of town and you constantly keep missing shows, chances are, I won't have any faith in you and won't take you seriously. And bragging is a big NEGATIVE. You should rather have someone boast on you because they see your accomplishments, rather than you telling them all about your accolades.

To me it just sounds silly to brag and you don't have anything to show for it. I think this is the thing that can stop an artist's career.

You don't have to lie your way to the top or fake it till you make it. This is a turn off. Even if there's some truth to what you're saying, let me see it for myself. You don't have to impress anyone by words.

If someone likes what you do, trust me they'll let you know. If you have to ask for feedback, it's one or two things, either they haven't listened to it or they didn't like it. They just didn't want to hurt your feelings. You can't force people to like your material you can only present it. They say that once you make it in the industry you start to change, sometimes for the good but most often for the worst.

I have seen people change just after they heard their song on the radio or if they have a good reaction off of the crowd. Nevertheless, there is some type of change you must go through to be successful.

Before you make it in the industry you must have discipline. You must be marketable and you must have good people behind you. I've learned so much in this industry and I'm not even on the big level yet.

For instance, I have seen good talent go to waste and I have seen something small become big. This has made me live my life differently.

I remember saying just 10 years ago, if I can make just $20 an hour or find a career, that's all I needed out of life. So after I surpassed my goal I realized that I was thinking very shallow and limiting myself.

Now yes, my life has improved and I'm making a good salary, however, the key is that I'm making someone very wealthy. NOW IT'S TIME TO INVEST IN ME! These days, my goals are a little different.

I don't think like the common man like working a 9 to 5 and hopefully having a retirement pension before I die. I'm trying to sell my dream by my music, books, and promotion.

I was once told to be successful in this world you must have seven ways of making money. That's something to think about if you only have one way. I realize it's easy to work a job and have that company chronicle your life till you retire. But let's think outside the box, lets put us in positions to achieve. There are people doing major transactions every minute of the day, we need to be a part of that percentage of people. We need to educate ourselves as well as set up a pathway to achieve our dreams.

There's nothing wrong with pursuing a rap career, but why not take a couple of business classes or some type class to help better yourself? I've been writing and rapping for a while but a few years ago I stopped rapping and writing to go back to school.

I also wanted to establish a career and start a family. Now, I've finished several schools, received a degree and several licenses in my field. I have some seniority on the job and have a family, then I went back to what I love, rapping and writing.

But now it's different, I have money to invest in my music, books, and promotions. I've built a studio to record, I have several published books and we have one of the longest most profitable Hip-hop showcases in St. Louis.

I couldn't have done this when I was younger. My mind wasn't right and I didn't have the type of money I have now. Even though I have more responsibilities with my family, it's still easier now to complete my dreams.

I used to work harder with lower wages. Now I work smarter with higher wages. Don't think that since you feel like you're the best artist that is going to make you successful. You need some type of formal education to make it in this world. I have 2 trades and one of my trades is Heating and cooling.

I still do side jobs involving HVAC; anything I can do to make a legitimate living. I'm on it. Even when I'm doing a Heating and cooling job, I'm letting the customer know about my books and music.

Just know that there are a lot of people that want that same break as you in the industry who may be just as good as you or even better. SO YOU HAVE TO BE TWICE AS GOOD AS YOUR COMPETITION!!

So, start off early in your career making good decisions that will set you up to achieve.

Networking

Networking is a little different than promoting. Even though it has the same concept, but you have to be more sociable when networking. Have you ever inquired about a job, car, or even something as little as shoes?

THAT'S NETWORKING! Networking is when you're inquiring or telling someone else about something that is useful. It's like giving information about someone or something.

In this industry, if you don't network you're not going to get very far. We network everyday, whether we like it or not. As artists, promoters, business owners etc. we need to promote twice as hard.

As an artist you should be networking with other artists or promoters to see about events that are happening. Also to see how they can help put your dreams in place. As a promoter, we should be networking with business owners to see about different ventures.

Furthermore, we should be making connections with the radio stations for different promotions they may have. As a club owner, we need to network with different promoters to have all club nights well promoted and packed.

This is just the tip of the iceberg, as far as networking everyday. I get calls everyday about the music and SO SHOULD YOU, IF YOU'RE SERIOUS. I network with people I have never met. I tell people about other events that are happening in my city or out of town. I wish everyone would grasp this concept. It seems like most promoters would like to have artists come to just their events.

IT SHOULDN'T BE THAT WAY, everyone needs to eat if they're serious about this industry. Why not tell an artist about every event especially if they're from out of town? I just wish that other promoters felt the same way.

If you tell out of town artists about every event in your city that you can think of, they'll love to come back. Now they'll spread the word about how many shows he or she did when they visited your city.

They would also have others come and visit. Now your name is out there and you're making money. My company is merging promotions with another known company. Every time you hear about their club night they're telling people about our club night.

THAT'S HOW YOU NETWORK! I support you and you support me. I have seen companies go under in this industry because of lack of networking. Instead they would rather COMPETE TO WIN.

THAT IS A NO NO IN THIS INDUSTRY. You might have success for a while, but it won't last. Why compete, let's go after one goal, TO HAVE EVERYONE WIN! You don't have to talk bad about another company just to get people to your events. You win people over by WORKING HARD, HAVING A SOLID PRODUCT, RUNNING YOUR COMPANY WITH INTEGRITY AND NETWORKING WITH OTHERS. I live by this guideline, that's why we have one of the longest running hip-hop showcases.

People will always have something to say about you whether it's good or bad. The key is to have more people saying positive things as opposed to negative things.

You as an artist have a product to sell. This product is your livelihood and you must sell it by all means necessary, but if you don't open your mouth, you'll never be a top seller. You may have people to handle that part, but if you're not selling a million in products, you may need to start NETWORKING.

I attend conferences and I see so many artists either empty handed or they're just passing out cd's. AND YOU WONDER WHY YOU HAVEN'T MADE IT TO THE TOP! You don't have to give a person your life story when you give them a cd, but a small conversation would help.

Introduce yourself; don't just interrupt that person saying you're the hottest artist in your city. THAT'S TACKY! After you introduce yourself try asking that person, what he or she does in the music industry. This gives them the spotlight and it makes it seem like you're doing the interview and research. You have to realize that these industry people deal with so many artists.

Whether the artists are good or bad, it's refreshing for someone to inquire about the A&R. That's when you give him/her your spiel, BUT DON'T OVER DO IT! More than likely the A&R will listen. You're there to inquire about support, while the A&R is there to see new talent.

When you network in a room with a lot of people you have to make your presence known. You can't just sit back and expect someone to come to you because you feel your music is good. So work on your personality as well as your speech.

I had a person call me about management, but he didn't have any type of game plan. I know that's what managers are for, but you have to know where you're going with your product. Try to work on your presentation also.

Networking is easy to people who love to talk. So if you're not one of those people learn how to be friendly and outgoing. When I'm out I wear our magazine/all access badge. This way, people can come to me inquiring about our magazine.

This is good for a person who's not sociable. Once you put that badge on people will want to inquire about you or ask questions about your badge.

That badge get's me into places were I need to be, so I can network with big name people. I can use the magazine as a trade value too. A magazine is good exposure for anyone.

So think about that the next time you have trouble fraternizing with people. You'll be surprised by the things you'll find out about a person or the connections he or she has.

You never know, the connection might benefit you, JUST OPEN YOUR MOUTH! There are people out there who are willing to help you and would enjoy doing so.

As time passes us by, so does technology. People advertise everywhere like on highway billboard signs or TV. The more and more you see this, the better the chances of a consumer purchasing the product.

We should be a walking billboard as well. This is a good form of networking and promoting your merchandise or company. This is also good for people who are nervous or shy when they talk to people.

Try to get a shirt made with pertinent info, like a number, website or social site. People like to research the product before they buy it. There are many forms of networking; some people use the internet as a tool for doing so.

Don't be afraid to use social sites for networking purposes. As mentioned previously, if you use this to your advantage you'll find that your product might move faster. With a social website you can also network globally. Two years ago an out of state artist overheard about my company on Myspace. We were having an event in Atlanta and she wanted to perform at the show.

She told me a couple of days prior that she wouldn't be able to make it. We kept in touch and I'd tell her about shows in my city and vice versa.

That's the importance of networking with people. Now we have another city in which to promote our artist or product. You just never know the type of info someone can give you that will actually help you in the long run.

She told me that she was going to have a big show in her city 8 months from then. That's a long time, but by us networking we were able to remember and we performed in her city at her showcase.

Now we have an out of town place to perform. Many artists come to us to do out of town shows. They see the video and they feel that we have a lot of out of town connections. Even though this is true, it wouldn't be possible without NETWORKING!

You have to reach out to artists or promote when you're on a social networking site. Listen to their music; you may want to do a collaboration with that artist. This is definitely another way of building solid connections.

When you're at a show and there are people from out of town, network with them. That's what we do; you already have something in common with them, music Out of town shows just don't fall in your lap. You have to network with people from other cities.

You have to be ready to go out of town and network. DON'T LET AN OPPORTUNITY LIKE THIS PASS YOU BY BECAUSE YOU'RE ILL PREPARED.

Don't make excuses about going out of town or about not being available to go out of town, especially if you want to make it in this industry. You have to be willing to go above the norm. Remember, there are artists in the same boat as you, who are willing and able to make those trips.

SO GUESS WHO WILL MAKE IT IN THIS INDUSTRY? The question now is; will it be you? Some artists come to us asking about out of town shows just to sell their product.

For most artists, when you tell them that the promoter doesn't have room on his list to perform, they don't want to go.

First off let me start by saying this, YOU SHOULD GO ANYWAY! You never know, there could be a couple of people on the list that won't show up. Besides, you never know, the promoter may let you perform anyway.

Plus, you should go to network; you might find someone there to invite you to another showcase. One thing's for sure, is that the best place to find a promoter that throws showcases is at a showcase networking. You might be able to sell a lot of cd's or have promotional gear for people to buy your product JUST DON'T GIVE UP BECAUSE YOU CAN'T PERFORM..

Network with different local businesses such as clothing stores, stereo shops, and barber shops. If the owner see's that you're consistent he or she may let you put posters up or let you leave promotional gear there.

If you're known, people might ask where you get your haircut or clothes from. You can tell them and when they go you'll have your cd's or product there where they can pick it up. Trust me, store owners see that and don't mind helping you out.

We have artists that come to our show that do concerts at this one clothing store because of their consistency. They have done videos as well. This drives people to their establishment, so they don't mind letting you do those types of things. Network with everybody. I even network with the CEO of my daytime job. He loves what we do. He was probably the same way before he created his company.

Don't get discouraged if people don't see your dreams. Some people are programmed to only know how to work for other people. Network with people that have similar dreams. It doesn't have to necessarily be anyone in the music business.

Maybe someone who wants to own their own business or strive to create something would be of great service to you and vice versa. He or she may have connections that you need or you may have connections to something they need. That's how people establish corporations through networking.

Networking is a universal language that everyone speaks. Like I said before, if everyone is eating, everyone is happy. What's the use of having big money if the people around you are suffering?

So put people in places where you know they will succeed, instead of just helping people out. Always give back to your community to help build other establishments. Seek people that like to help others.

Let's restore our youth to help them build strong networking markets. There's more to life then to work for people that have big money. If you have a good proposal or a scope of work, let's look for sponsorships or a different way of running your company. You may have a good business that's small, but until you put the proper touch to your company, it would stay SMALL.

A lot of times big corporations want to reach out to the smaller companies because they like what they do and they started out the same way. As a small business, we don't know how to get the proper help because we think small.

It takes money to make money. That might be all it takes to succeed in the industry. A lot of big businesses would like to have promoters reach out to the people for their business.

One reason, promoters are close to the streets, is if you have flyers, most of the big businesses just want to have their logo on the flyers as a sponsor.

Don't be scared to go after important sponsors if you have a good business practice. Every time we have a big show we offer sponsors V.I.P, free guest and a page in our magazine and in most cases a bottle of champagne.

Whether you're a big company or small, ALL PROMOTION IS GOOD PROMOTION, so don't limit yourself. If you think small you'll stay small. Remember, every business owner had to start some where and it wasn't at the top.

Just create good networking resources and have integrity in everything you do and you'll find yourself living the dream. Even if you can't find a big sponsor, try to find a sponsor. This could be anyone wanting to invest money in your business. The best type of sponsor in this industry is an artist.

If you can put their picture or logo on a flyer, most artists will pay for that. This isn't costing you a dime. We have added artists to our radio commercial for our shows. We offer V.I.P with free guest as well as recognition on our flyers.

THAT'S EXPOSURE! An artist doesn't mind paying for that especially when he knows how we promote. We have promoted so many artists through networking, it's almost unbelievable to people who don't know our company.

Now you have to figure out how you can offer a service to get sponsors. Once you have a sponsor, it's easier to get more. A good legitimate sponsor is concerned with the integrity of your company. They don't want to tack their name on something they don't believe in or anything that's going to damage their name.

If your business is good, prove it to these sponsors with paperwork or word of mouth. If your business is not the way you want it to be, strive to make it better before you seek a sponsor.

Sponsors are out there, you just need the proper tools for them to invest in your company. Like I said before, everyone has to start from some where. If a sponsor sees your effort, most of them are willing to invest in some way. So, invite them to your event or let them view your product, so they can see why you're working so hard to achieve your dream.

You may get a lot of sponsors saying no before you'll get a yes, but don't let that discourage you. Create a strong following of friends. This will help you to promote your product. Don't be afraid to network through your community and families as well.

They can be your biggest sellers. At every family reunion I score big, because I always have a book that comes out around that time. Family loves to support especially for a good reason.

I also network through schools, church etc. I used to teach at a college and I would network between the students about a show or my personal product. The school would let me post my material in the student and staffs break room. I got a lot of exposure throughout the campus.

Networking is the wave of the future; in most cases it can be more effective than most physical advertisement. You'll be amazed to hear where people seen or heard your advertisement. When you include people in your movement that's FREE PROMOTION!

This is how corporations are started. If you're not networking with others you might be left behind. Networking is easy because it can be done on a daily basis without much thought.

Managing Artists

Everyone loves music, whether for relaxing or making it. Some of us are fortunate to be in the industry following our love. Even if you're not musically inclined, THERE IS STILL A JOB FOR YOU! Most people love the idea of discovering new talent or helping someone with their talent.

But remember, however great your intentions may be, there is a possibility that you can damage an artist's career if you don't know what you're doing. I think with any job or position you should be properly trained.

Most of us just jump into the manager position with no experience. You might have a good run and you might be the motivation that artist needs, but that's just a fraction of the responsibility you need in order to successfully manage an artist.

Think of an artist as a painting, you have to do the work for it to become a masterpiece. The artist's job is to show what he represents to the world. Everyone needs someone to manage them or some type of representation to be successful.

An artist should focus on his craft and the manager should focus on the business. We get so many artists wanting us to represent them, but it's not a simple process. It takes time to sign an artist to our management company. We need to believe in you just as much as you need to believe in us. What if we signed an artist because we seen him or her perform a couple of times, but we weren't compatible with that artists' style of music. Moreover, we need to follow your lifestyle to see if you're serious about your music.

We need to see if you're a fit. You should be critiquing us also. That process can take some time. Just because you hear good things about us or you see how we manage our artists doesn't mean we are right for you and vice versa.

You can't assume we're going to be the best fit for you. Believe me; we go through trials and tribulations with managing our artists. The promotion side is easier, but our love for music and good talent gives us a passion for this business.

That's what keeps us going. THIS IS NOT A GAME! You can make a good living off of your music, the kind of living where you don't need a 9 to 5. Being a manager, you are the direct link to the artist.

Anything that the artist accomplishes, be it good or bad, represents you. Choosing the right artist is essential. Don't just manage an artist because he makes good music. That should be one of the last reasons.

So now you need to know the artist's personality and business sense. You want an artist who knows what's going on, but not an artist that thinks he or she knows everything. This is a growing experience, you and your artist need to be open minded and receptive to different things.

Don't be afraid to learn new things or think that you're more knowledgeable than everyone else because you've been doing this longer. YOU CAN ALWAYS LEARN SOMETHING FROM ANYONE AT ANY GIVEN TIME! Being a manager, I know the needs of different artists.

Becoming a manager is more than just dealing with music. You must be a mentor as well as manage their music. Remember, there's not such a thing as a perfect artist. When you deal with artists you become a part of their life.

Regardless if the artist's life is good or bad, YOU HAVE TO DEAL WITH IT. You have to be the middle man between the music and real life for your artist. Most artists rap about what's going on in their lives.

If they're selling drugs, committing crimes or using drugs, you have to put them on the right track in order for them to be successful. The artist depends on you to make their dreams become reality. They depend on you to get the best deals or to handle their music business.

People don't realize this until it's too late and a lot of relationships are ruined because of the stress, but you want the best for your artist and yourself, so you have to lay down the rules and deadlines. You have to be on point.

Once a label is interested in your artist, you can't slack off or have your artist slacking. So if you lay the rules down early, your artist will be ready for any challenge.

The artist represents you in everything they do. If their music is good or bad your name is getting mentioned, SO, DO YOUR HOMEWORK ON THESE ARTISTS BEFORE YOU DECIDE TO SIGN THEM! I received my experience managing one of our artists when I first joined the management team.

It was a different experience because I'm an artist myself and I had to put my plans on the shelf to promote our new artist. I found out that the reward is great when the artist has a successful show, but it's a lot of work getting there.

Our artist went through a lot of personal problems and I found myself right there with him at times. Like I said before, it's not just about the music. You have to make sure his material is right before he tries to sell it to people.

If he or she doesn't have the money, you have to chip in. Everything in this industry consists of being at the right place at the right time and having the right resources. Sometimes you have to motivate the artist. We used to tell them that they should want success twice as much as we want them to succeed.

Artists need to have discipline too. If they need to be at a show at a certain time, it's your job to make sure they're on time, especially if it's a paid show. I used to pick my artist up to make sure he was on time, even if it's out of the way.

YOU HAVE TO SACRIFICE! At the beginning of any contract with an artist, most of the time there's no money involved because you're trying to find a deal. Also, the artist is unknown and it's up to you to let the world see or hear his talent.

So a budget is necessary to survive, because it costs to be seen and heard. DON'T LET MONEY BE YOUR DOWN FALL! Keeping an artist on track is one of the most COMPLICATED things to do, because, you have to live your life, especially if you have a family to provide for.

When an artist has personal problems it makes it harder to complete the mission. That's a lot of stress to deal with. Your family is on you, you're trying to get your artist right and life still has to go on.

Your day job is giving you stress. WHO WANT TO BECOME A MANAGER NOW? There is a reward called LOYALTY, but every one is not loyal, even after the hard work you put in. So choose your artists wisely.

I didn't realize the work it took to manage an artist when I first got into this industry. So I had a crash course. There've been times when I got so frustrated that I wanted to give up, but I can't because I have people depending on me.

I had to give my last to get items needed for the artist. Motivate the artist to go on out of town trips. Even if you have to pay for the artist to go out of town if he or she is broke, you must do this. Remember, you're a star out of town.

The best part about this deal is that I HAVEN'T RECEIVED ONE DIME FOR MY WORK YET! Our artist hasn't been signed yet, so there is no money coming in. DON'T GET DISCOURAGED, THE MONEY WILL COME. Still interested? Still interested? Then read on!

Build a strong foundation first and then worry about the money later. You don't want to get the money first and then everything starts to fall apart. Imagine if that was your day job. Your boss told you to work hard and one day we might get that big contract and I can finally pay you for your hard work.

You'll probably look at him like he was crazy. Managers do this everyday, hoping for their dreams to come true and most of the time IT DOESN'T! This is a very risky game that only the strong survive.

I have seen them come and go on the promotion side as well as the management side. Before you get in this field as a manager, do your research. Most management company doesn't survive the first year let alone survive maintaining an artist.

THAT'S A FACT; I HAVE SEEN IT WITH MY VERY OWN EYES. If you advertise about management your going to get a lot of inquires. Artists feel that's their next step to getting that major deal.

You have to distinguish between the real artists and the fake artists. The fake artist may tell you how their music is

the best and every label wants them but they lack the
discipline and energy to put forth quality work.

They may tell you about all the shows they did out of
town and that their song is playing on the radio, but you've
never heard it. They may also say that they sold so many
copies of their cd, but don't have one to give you.

All of this with no proof. AND THEY WONDER WHY
PEOPLE DON'T TAKE THEM SERIOUS! A real artist
would want to know more about you and your company.
They don't need to tell you about the different labels that
want to sign them.

The real artist knows that it's irrelevant if he or she isn't
signed. The real artist isn't going to tell you that his or her
song is on the radio because they're smart enough to know
that information is very easy to verify.

Most real artists will direct you to a social website, so that
you can see their shows and view counts, also, if a real
artist tells you about his independent record sells, he or she
will have promotional gear and a cd to give you.

A real artist knows the first thing a manager who's
interested, just wants to hear their music. Basically, a
REAL ARTIST DOESN'T HAVE TO LIE TO GET
NOTICED.

In my city most artists feel that you have to go out of
town to get signed to a major deal.

I don't know about that, but you must go out of town to make new fans. I don't understand when artist always make excuses about going out of town. When you get signed you spend most of your time going from city to city doing shows.

If you're not comfortable going out of town you're going to have problems. Sometimes you have to leave town with no warning. If someone wants you to headline a show, that's a perfect opportunity, so don't waste it.

Most of an artist's money comes from performing at paid shows, so how can you turn down something you love doing that PAYS? The internet is a great way to get peoples support in state and out of state.

Everyone is not on the internet and some people want to see a live performance to feel the energy, before buying your product. We try to go out of town at least once every two months to our artist's shows.

We go to Atlanta so much that people think we live there. We also film to show people our progress, even if it's just going out of town to promote. You can always meet a contact person to get you shows in their town.

Sometimes motivating your artists to go out of town is a challenge, but it must be done. We use our shows to generate money to pay for the rental and the hotel just so our artists can have a more definitive plan when traveling out of town.

That's how important it is to go out of town. It's a sacrifice, but you must do it. That's how we were able to do a yearly show in Atlanta as well as buying into HOT BLOCK MAGAZINE!

If you know that an artist is out of town from your city, NETWORK WITH THEM! If you can get a lot of people to go out of town with you, it will cut down on the cost. It will also, make driving a lot easier.

Going out of town is a good experience for any artist. You get to network with a lot of people who share the same passion. I realized that in this independent music game, everyone deals with the same success, drama, and work habits.

We've all seen the Keyshia Cole show, about how her manager Manny handles her everyday business, or how Diddy has everyone working for him, BUT WE'RE NOT AT THAT LEVEL YET!

Many artists think that the managers are supposed to do everything the artist says, but how is that possible when there's no money being made? THE OBJECT IS TO SELL ALBUMS! I can't stress this enough.

It seems like artist forget that they need fans to buy their music. A fan is worth more than anything in the music industry because they're who creates capitol. We need to work together to accomplish one common goal, TO SELL ALBUMS!

We had an artist in the past that admitted he had the big head when he started to get popular. He wanted to charge people to have him featured on their songs. That's fine if you're a big name, but he was in the same situation as any other artist.

You should try to be on any type of promotion to get your name out there. What if that artist is serious about his music or had connections but didn't have the money for you to be on his new song?

That's a missed opportunity. He had the big head until a popular artist did the same thing to him. Even if someone is willing to pay you for being on their song, it could still be a little resentment from that artist, especially if you're friends with the artist.

I know there's a thin line between friendship and business, but remember you need to create more fans than enemies. I don't understand how you can get the big head when you're in the same spot you're in when you stepped into the game.

Just because your song is on the radio doesn't make you an overnight celebrity. If you go out of town you'll get a reality check.

You'll see how a lot of underground rappers have a movement stronger than most artists that are signed. BUT THEY'RE STILL HUMBLE. Being a manger, you have to be in tuned with the genre of music your artist is in.

Sometimes a manager can miss an opportunity by not understanding different musical concepts. We had this one group that would always come to our show, so we would put them on all of our flyers.

As time went by we hadn't heard from them, so one day they called wanting to know about a show we were throwing. They wanted us to talk to their new manager to bring him up-to-date. He was an older guy, so we told him the basic concepts of our show.

We also told him that we like to put the artist's picture on our flyers to help them out with promotions. He started talking about being compensated for having his group on our flyers to bring people in the club.

By him being new and not knowing anything about Hip-hop, he probably doesn't listen to Hip-hop. We had to explain to him that this is an open mic event and the artist doesn't bring people because most of the crowd is artists.

When we put artists on our flyers, we are helping that artist promote, we don't need to put them on the flyers. We have our own artists to promote; we just like to give back to everyone that supports us.

He understood, but this is a prime example of why you can't just assume every manager is knowledgeable or every artist is a good fit. Sometimes artists need to look at themselves, before they look for management. A manager can weed out an artist who's not motivated.

You don't have to lie in order to have a manager. Sometimes managers put you on a trial period before they even sign you.

So don't think that just because your single is hot a manager will automatically sign, you. You have to show and prove. If you have a lot of personal problems or something is always holding you back, don't assume that getting a manager will automatically smooth everything out.

Understand that a manager is here to help push your career, NOT TO BABYSIT. This one artist that lives out of state inquired about management, so we invited him to our show. Remember, he's looking for management, not us.

He never came to our show, but I would get phone calls about how well his song was doing in his area. He suggested that we need to manage him because he has a couple of deals on the table from different labels.

We never met him, because he never came to a show. So we're supposed to drop everything to pursue him and his dreams just because he said so? Let's discover the right way to handle business because that AIN'T it!

If you can't come to shows, go out of town, or don't have cd's to sell or pass out, you need to go back to the basics. Don't waste anybody's time thinking that your ready for the next level when clearly, you're not! We even had out of town shows near his home town but he never came to out.

Like I said before, our first step is to see your performance and hear your music even if it's not at our showcase.

That was never established. Time went on and we lost communication with him again. One day he called and was in the same position he was in about a year ago asking the same questions as before.

What happened to the deals you had on the table or your song being heard on the radio? He was either lying or lazy and a good manager can see through those clouds. SO WHY LIE TO PEOPLE?

If you're having major movement, you should be able to do shows out of town. When you get signed and you're in demand you're going to have to do out of town show on limited notice. You might as well practice now.

We get so many artists looking for management, but they're not prepared to be managed. Remember, actions speak volumes, so let me make a decision off of your movement or action, not based on what you say.

You shouldn't have to tell a person that you work so hard to sell your product; they should see your progress. You don't hear people in the industry brag about what they do; let the media do it for them. Think about preparing yourself first before you go in search of a manager. Choosing the right manager can determine your career, so you should do your research and prepare yourself

A good manager can only help you; he or she can't hurt you. Everyone has that one cousin or brother that can rap or has that daughter or sister that can sing. Basically someone has a member of their family that has talent.

Everyone heard of the horror stories about the industry or how managers can take the artists' money due to a bad contract, so you want to step in since you are the older family member or mom or dad to take the place of a manager to protect their best interest.

This is noble; however, YOU HAVE NO EXPERIENCE! This can hurt their career. I have seen it happen. Let a manager who has been in the game do the job. You can certainly oversee the project but leave the management side to the professionals. This is a job and just like the corporate world you wouldn't give the job to someone that's not qualified or don't have a clue about the position

Having your family members' interest is one thing, but when it comes down to getting signed and handling contracts, you need to let someone who is experienced deal with it.

Just because the artist feels they're the hottest thing around, THE INDUSTRY MAY OR MAY NOT AGREE! Then you as a relative start to take it personal and can really jeopardize their career. This is about business, not feelings! Although there are snakes in the industry, there are many others who are willing and able to get the job done. You just have to find them, SO LET THE PROFESSIONALS

DO THEIR JOB! Sometimes as a relative taking on a manager's position, you might not take the time to learn the music business, like booking shows etc. When you deal with a promoter his or her time could be limited.

You need to know the right questions to ask instead of wasting valuable time. For instance, go to a couple of shows first to see how they operate before you try to book a show for your artist.

You might answer a lot of questions just by observing. If you're a parent of an artist, get info on how to manage before you make a decision that can hurt your son or daughters career. I knew this guy that had a group that consisted of 2 boys.

He would book their shows, write some of their lyrics and put the necessary funds up to get their promotional gear. HE WAS LEADING THEM IN THE RIGHT DIRECTION AS THEIR MANAGER.

The group made good music as well. I would always see them out promoting and would see them at a lot of different shows. People started to notice them, so they were on the way to bigger and better things, but one day their parents decided to go with another company because they had a bigger name.

There's nothing wrong with that. You always want what's best for your kids, but in this case, they went about it the wrong way.

Not to mention, there wasn't any paper work signed because it was a favor. This kind of thing can happen to anyone lacking the necessary experience. They didn't realize that their actions impacted others.

The previous manager had to find out from someone else that he no longer managed the duo. So now that same group hasn't been sited at any shows, no one see's them promoting like they used to do. It's as if they're fallen off.

That's what happens when inexperienced people try to manage other people's careers. Not to mention, you could have breached contract and been held liable for those actions.

There's nothing wrong with getting someone else, but do your homework and go about it the right way. The person who you decided to get might be the snake you were trying to keep your family member away from.

If someone is working hard on your behalf, at least give them the courtesy of being involved with the decision making.

How to Spot Talent

Music has evolved to a point where everyone wants to get in the business. Now it's easy with home studios, duplication equipment, internet etc. Now you can make your own music and distribute it because of all of the technology we have today.

The industry expects more from artists as far as quality of their product. Talent is more than just being able to rap or sing. To stay ahead of the game, you must be versatile. You have artists who can make beats, record and mix their own products.

Some artists can go as far as to master their music too. With the use of a web cam or camcorder, artists can upload their video on the web and have millions to see it. With a little bit of ingenuity and technology, artists are getting signed to major deals.

Many artists are selling their music worldwide. When I look for an artist, if their music is good they have my curiosity.

Now I need to look at their personal life to see how that's going. A person can tell you a lot about themselves just by talking to them. You want a person who's confident but not arrogant, and who listens and can take constructive criticism. I like to see if an artist is compatible with other artists. A good artist can and should be able to work with anybody.

Talent is something that should come naturally. Some artists have that natural ability, but their attitude kills it for them.

For other artists they have to work harder at developing their ability because they lack a little talent. I listen to how artists put songs together and how they arrange songs on their album or mix tape.

A good song should consist of a catchy hook, a good beat, and the most important element is GOOD LYRICS. A lot of artists have good music that never gets heard.

It's hard to get recognition, but it can be done. When you put a mixtape or album together you have to know how to arrange the songs. Most people only listen to the first couple of minutes of an album or mixtape before they decide to listen to the rest of it.

So you have to have your hit songs at the beginning as well as the end. Good artwork also attracts people to your cd. I cannot say this enough about artists that don't spend the money or time to make their product presentable.

For the amount of time you spent creating the product, to the producers used, to the actual recording; to have someone take one look at your cd and throw it away CAN BE DEVASTATING! Just remember, the time and effort you put into your product is sometimes equivalent to what you get in return. This happens all the time. Like I said so many times before, APPEARANCE IS EVERYTHING.

So don't slack up on graphics on your product because of money, just save up and get everything done the right way. Trust me IT MAKES A DIFFERENCE. I've heard many cd's that sounded very good but just had a name scribbled on it.

Most people wouldn't even listen to it because the artist didn't take the time to get everything done the proper way. If an artist has everything together and is serious about his music, he or she is definitely a great candidate.

So now you want to go in depth with his music and performance. You've seen them perform and it wasn't what you expected. It wasn't bad, but it wasn't up to par. You must put him through some type of artist development.

This could just be the artist watching other good artists perform or getting singing lessons. Stage presence is very important because you want to have your fans feeling what you're doing on stage.

If you can control your audience than you definitely have stage presence. You can be a very good singer or the best lyricist, but if your stage presence is bad you can lose fans, it happens more often than you can imagine.

Major artists make their money mostly off of touring and performing and not off of album sales. A bad performance can literally end your career. You must know how to work the stage and perform to your fans and not to yourself. We had a group of young artists come to our show to perform.

It was about 8 in the group. When they performed they put all the focus on themselves. There wasn't any eye contact with the crowd and they were looking at each other while they performed.

The crowd lost interest in their performance because they were rapping to each other instead of rapping to the audience. Even if you have a good song, when you perform live your audience would like to be entertained. After their performance, they asked me how they did. They were commenting that they were hype and running around the stage.

I told them that I liked the song, but they lost the crowd. The audience is there to be entertained and you guys were entertaining each other. Next time, put the focus and energy toward the crowd and watch their reaction. Just because you were yelling on the mic and running around on the stage doesn't mean that the audience felt the same way.

This next artist was the exact opposite. He would come to our shows and win the cash prize regularly. When he performed he got the audience involved.

He had a great hook and an even greater delivery. To top that off he had a dance that everyone loved doing the minute his song came on.

By having a catchy hook, it makes people want to sing every time they hear it. Even from people that don't know him, they're singing his song.

When he performs, he commands you to listen to what he has to say. A person with a good stage performance can make people get up from their seats and move toward the stage just to see the performance. Or go to the dance floor to dance just to your song.

That's how you perform a song. You shouldn't have to ask if your performance was good. People should be coming to you asking for a cd or when is your next show. Think about that the next time you're in the studio.

If you choose a job where you're in the spotlight, whether you're an artist, reporter, or an actor, you need to have an image. In today's society image is everything. Some people may not have the talent but their image is what the industry is looking for.

I have known people with great talent but the image is what's stopping them from taking that next step. For example, the story about Jermaine Dupree finding his group KrissKross at the mall.

They were average kids, but he saw their image. He turned these average kids into a multi platinum selling group. THAT'S WHAT IMAGE IS. An artist is not just a person who makes music.

He or she is a role model. A lot of kids have fantasies about living the life of an artist, or having a crush on the artist. The music industry acts on these dreams by producing a megastar that lives up to everyone's

Satisfaction. The reward is stardom and money. There may be a couple of artist that slipped by because of their music, but they might not have the same success as an artist with a good image. Some people may like a person's song because of their image.

So work on your image because the first impression may be the last impression. People are often judged based on their image. If you're seen with a certain crowd that likes doing bad things you may be viewed as the same.

Just work on your own image and try to stand out in front of your competition. Some people may purchase a product because of the person who's endorsing it. They might not even care for the product that much. THAT'S POWERFUL. The good thing about a person's image is that you work on bringing your image up to standard.

Get in tune to what is happening in today's society; find out what people like as far as style and music and remember, once your image is set and you become popular you're now in the spotlight.

Things you used to be able to get away with may be a little harder now since all eyes are on you. So you definitely have to think a little smarter. Sometimes friends don't understand this concept especially the one's that do dirt.

If you and your friends used to get into trouble, YOU NEED TO STOP! Especially if a record label or sponsor put money into your career, they don't want you to be a bad investment. You might have to let your friends go or run the risk of being let go.

I know it's hard, but this is your dream and you must uphold your image, so protect it at all costs. Don't let anyone take your dream away. In this business there are a lot of snakes and predators. Some of them you'll see and some may sneak up on you.

Once your image is damaged it's very difficult to get it back in good standards depending on what happened. So be smart, avoid trouble and surround yourself with good people.

You never know who's ready to test your good image. Think of your image as your life line and if you damage your image, that can be the end of your career.

When I pay attention to songs I like to listen to the lyrics. That may be a little old fashioned, but to me that's where music begins. So, an artist with good lyrics will always get my attention.

I feel that an artist that has a nice flow and good lyrics but lack good production is easy to work with rather than a artist that sounds good due to good production. There are a lot of good producers, engineers, and good studios out there. Talent is something that is GOD given. I know in today's society if you have a good producer with a good sound and you have that one single that everyone loves,

you really don't need talent for your music to sale.
Most artists in that category don't have LONGEVITY in
this industry. Even though I said before that it's about 70%
business and 30% music, but remember, the business aspect
is made up on music, so music is were it begins.

In my opinion you can work on a person's image, weight,
age, and music. The next time someone tells you that
you're too old or your image is bad, DON'T GIVE UP.
The one thing a person cannot stop is GOOD MUSIC!

If you make good music, everything else is extraneous.
There are millions of artists that have GOOD MUSIC, that
haven't been discovered, and there are a lot of artist who
have ok music that is making a living off of it.

It depends on the level of success you want to achieve.
Music is universal, there isn't one person in the world that
don't like some form of music. Use that to your advantage.
Every artist that you meet wants to go to the next level in
their music career, but 90% of the artists are not ready.

So you have to decide if you want to spend the time
developing an artist who's not ready but you feel that he or
she is worth it, or do you want the full package in an artist
that's ready to get the deal.

Preparing for a Major Deal

Now the time has come, you've prepared your artist for a major deal; you're shopping from label to label hoping an A&R will notice. Your artists' music sounds excellent and they've learned how to rock a crowd.

When people look at your artist they think he or she is in the music industry. Your artist has gained loyal fans. THE INDUSTRY NEEDS TO PREPARE FOR THEIR IMPACT RIGHT? THERE'S JUST ONE THING THAT'S STOPPING YOUR TRIUMP!

THE PART ABOUT KNOWING THE MUSIC BUSINESS! Most labels, executives, and A&R's are very busy, so to catch their attention you need to be FAST and always to the POINT.

You have done everything to put your artist on the right track, now it's time to transform your hard work into industry standards.

YOU MUST BE PREPARED! Do your research before you make it to this point. This might be a once in a lifetime chance. DON'T BLOW YOUR OPPORTUNITY BY NOT BEING PREPARED!

Remember, there are millions of artists out there that are unheard of and there are the very few that are signed and actually are doing well in the industry. Being prepared means everything to a starving artist. Having a demo cd is great, but that's just the tip of the iceberg. Make sure there are anywhere from 3-5 songs and the 1st song should be your single or best song to catch the A&R's attention. If they like it, they may want to go a step further.

Along with your demo you should have a package that contain a one sheet bio, a 8x12 picture of the artist, a EPK and any type of promo gear that features the artist. A flyer and magazine clipping can be used as well.

Record labels want to assure themselves that they're making the right choice if they decide to sign you. You have to give them a reason why they should sign you out of the rest. Have your package professionally done.

Hire a professional photographer and do a couple of photo shoots. I'm the type of person that doesn't like taking pictures, but I had to change my feelings about that quickly. If you want to make it in this industry you must love to be in front of a camera.

A lot of people judge success by how many times they see your face on different thing. You must be able to take many photos.

Trust me it pays off. We take different poses for each flyer; we have so many shows were constantly having photo shoots. Our faces are everywhere. One of the most rewarding things I've accomplished when I first started was when I was out of town and this guy came up to me and said, "I've seen you before, I can't remember where though." Then he said my name and he opened his backpack and pulled out our magazine with or face on the front cover.

Even though people may not come up to you like he did me, it doesn't mean they don't see you and your progress, especially if your face is on flyers, DVD's, magazines, and other type of promotional paraphernalia.

SO GET USE TO IT, once you become famous you're going to be in front of a camera all the time for every little thing.

You're at the stage in your life where you have to take things serious. People see your ability that you posses, so the snakes in the industry start to show their faces. Let's educate ourselves on the music business side of this industry.

People say that the first major deal that you'll sign will be a bad deal. Let's understand why before we go in this deal blind.

Most deals, you're paying back everyone like the producers, engineers, label, distributions, promotion, and the small percent that's left goes to you, whatever that may be. Just imagine if your album flopped. That's when your label decides if they want to keep investing in you or not. All of the people that had a hand in your project either received their money from the label or will receive their money after the album debut. Let's go to the label prepared, take some music business classes to understand what goes on in the industry.

Don't just trust anything someone in a high position tells you. You might want to consult with a lawyer as well.

Any type of legal advice is good advice. Once you sign those papers you're entitled to fulfill the contract. In today's music world a lot of artists are multi-talented.

They're making their own beats, some artists sing and rap, or some artists know how to record themselves as well as duplicate their own products.

Some people say that home recording studios make it too easy for artists. I say use it to your advantage. If it's out there USE IT. Some years ago when I started rapping, I didn't have a clue about the Industry.

I didn't know how to record, make beats, or even how to COUNT BARS. I JUST KNEW HOW TO RAP. I didn't have the best paying job at the time, but I was finding out that everything was expensive. Like recording, buying beats, mastering fee, artwork, and making copies of the cd.

I wanted to cut down on some of the cost, so I went to music school. My plan was to learn how to make beats and learn the equipment, so I can at least make my own beats. I also wanted to identify quality equipment better. Little did I know I was learning how to make beats, record, master and learn how to use the equipment. With that under my belt, I decided to build my own studio and piece by piece I purchased the equipment I needed by taking on a second job at a local music store. This allowed me to make my purchases at drastically discounted rates.

So now I'm able to record, make beats, mix, and duplicate my own music. I have produced 3 albums out of my studio which sounds pretty good. I even make beats and record other people.

Be more than just an artist; control your fate in this industry. If you have to take classes, do it. You never know, you might find something else in this industry that's more rewarding.

There are people that made that change from being in front of the mic to being behind the mic. You'll find that you can be very successful and have the potential to make a lot of money in these different fields.

I DON'T WANT TO DISCOURAGE YOUR DREAMS; I'M JUST GIVING YOU OPTIONS. It's so much to know about the industry that may cause you problems if you don't know or understand.

THERE IS NO EXCUSE WHEN IT COMES TO IGNORANCE. Get involved with your music project and ask questions. When you're in the studio, instead of waiting while the engineer is mixing your song try to see what's he or she doing.

Sometimes if you ask questions, most people wouldn't mind explaining or teaching you. Software and equipment are easy to come by. Try practicing to get a feel for it. Anything that can help you to produce your product is a plus.

I used to go to the studio and I wouldn't even understand what they were saying until I started practicing and taking classes. It's too many people that are talented for you to just rap or sing.

A label may want to sign you to a production deal because you developed your beat making skills. That's your foot in the door; you may want to pursue that instead rapping or singing.

You can definitely make money as a producer. The way the world is going everyone is at a fast pace, we don't have time for anything. That's how we need to treat our presentation to the A&R's of a major label.

One of the quickest and easiest ways of presenting yourself is an EPK or Electronic Press Kit. A couple of months ago I was networking with this guy that managed a couple of groups who had major deals.

He was very open about what he does. Basically he had some good connections to get people in the right places. I was talking to him about our artist and one thing he kept mentioning was to send him our artist EPK. It was like every other word, he kept mentioning that.

Finally, he told me that with an EPK, it's all the info someone needs. An EPK is like a website or e-mail which usually contain a Bio, Music clips, Press photo, Tour dates, Promotional video, Website links, Press reviews and interviews, and contact info.

You can use a cd, DVD video, audio cassette, internet or even a flash drive to distribute your EPK. This is the industry standard when you're shopping around for a deal. The guidelines are simple and it's easy to put together.

But I suggest you get one done professionally. Don't get over looked because of your presentation not being up to standard. Remember you're competing for a slot that everyone wants. Keep in mind there are a lot of artist that have money.

Or the people behind the artist that has money, so you're in competition with that as well. They have the money to get professional videos, a street team to pass out their promotional gear, and able to pay to headline big shows,

BUT YOU HAVE TO THINK SMARTER! In the music industry, time moves at the speed of light. Most artists put their all into their music to get signed.

But after a while THEY STOP. Everyone needs some type of break or a period to refocus. Maybe some artists need time to develop their skills, stage presence, or music. NEVERTHELESS, TIME STOPS FOR NO ONE! As you take that much needed break, a new artist has emerged from out of the blue to pass you up. That new artist is hungrier; more developed, and have people helping them to get where they want to be. That artist is ready! All of this happened while you fell off.

I have seen the best of the best quit. I've seen the type of artist that you knew was going to make it QUIT! There's a point in every artist's life where they want to give up or has given up. Now your mind is clear and you want to come back but don't know how. You have burned bridges with your old connections, manager, label, and most importantly, YOUR FANS!

Even the one's that come back sometimes realize that it's not the same, people treat you differently because they figure that you'll just quit again. CAN YOU BLAME THEM? Now you're blaming everyone else for your wrong doings and short comings.

What you don't realize is that while you took that break or quit, WE DIDN'T and life moved on. You might have been the best on a label or the best performer, but now you have to start from the beginning because music priorities have changed.

If you took a couple years off and you're ready to come back GUESS WHAT, YOU'RE OLDER NOW! You're not the young sensation that everyone was after. Now you're like everyone else. YOU HAD A GREAT START, BUT FADED OFF IN THE SUNSET. SO WHAT'S NEXT?

Well there's hope after all but it takes more work than you did before you decided to quit. You have the option to become an independent artist if you'd like. This has really been the wave of the industry, even back in the days of TOO SHORT, BROTHA LYNCH HUNG AND TECH9NE selling their products and making a good living for themselves.

Actually a major label would rather see your fan buzz and independent sales before they sign you. AGAIN, THIS TAKES WORK! You have to make a name for yourself, you have to get in these streets and sell your product.

Basically, you HAVE TO GET FANS TO BUY YOUR MUSIC! With the internet you have sites like songcast and reverbnation that will let you sell your music on the web as an independent artist or label.

You can reach people overseas. Artists are getting signed off of social networking sites because of their fan base buzz. You can make a living off of your independent status and keep 100% of your money earned.

It's easier to set up independent labels now. There's a world of opportunity waiting for you, but you have to grab it. MY MUSIC IS DONE, WHAT'S NEXT? An industry waiting for your arrival because now you're READY!

THANK YOU FOR YOUR SUPPORT!!!

www.ingramcontent.com/pod-product-compliance
Lightning Source LLC
Chambersburg PA
CBHW072207280526
45788CB00002B/909